Isaac N. VanMeter

Pocket Hymns - Original and Selected

designed for the use of the Regular Baptist Church, and all who love our Lord Jesus Christ

Isaac N. VanMeter

Pocket Hymns - Original and Selected
designed for the use of the Regular Baptist Church, and all who love our Lord Jesus Christ

ISBN/EAN: 9783337089627

Printed in Europe, USA, Canada, Australia, Japan

Cover: Foto ©Lupo / pixelio.de

More available books at **www.hansebooks.com**

POCKET HYMNS.

ORIGINAL AND SELECTED.

DESIGNED FOR THE USE OF THE

REGULAR BAPTIST CHURCH,

AND ALL WHO LOVE OUR LORD JESUS CHRIST.

By ISAAC N. VANMETER,

OF MACOMB, ILLINOIS,

ELDER OF THE REGULAR BAPTIST CHURCH.

"I will sing unto the Lord as long as I live."

GALESBURG, ILL.:
REGISTER PRINTING HOUSE.
1867.

PREFACE

In presenting this little volume of Hymns to the Churches of Jesus Christ, and to the lovers of our Savior throughout our Country, the Compiler deems it proper to offer some of the reasons which have led him to do so, and to make a few explanatory remarks.

So far as he is acquainted, there is no such a work to be found among our churches, North or South, as this little volume claims to be—*small, cheap, convenient for the pocket, and of good paper and print, suitable for weak eyes; and, which is more important, in harmony with God's word and the teaching of the Holy Spirit.* True, there are some small selections of Hymns and Poems before the public; but, so far as his knowledge and judgment extend, the publisher believes that they contain much matter that no orthodox or intelligent Christian could either sing or sanction—it being contrary to sound doctrine. Our denomination are supplied with several *large collections*, such as *Beebe's, Clark's, Thompson's, Lloyd's, Butler's*, &c.; some of which are excellent selections, and should be found in every family; yet, such a little volume as is here presented has, hitherto, not been published. The want of such a work has long been felt by our churches and ministers, in the United States, and the compiler has been urged by brethren, for many years, to prepare such a little volume for the press. During the past season, he met, in his travels, with many able brethren, who solicited him to make the selection at once; and so, after much reflection and solemn prayer for direction, he undertook the task. Among other reasons, not necessary to mention, why the compiler, instead of some more competent person, has been requested to prepare the work for the press was, that many have desired too see a few of his original Hymns interspersed through the work, and because he has been, for several years, unable to perform manual labor, and could, therefore, find a little leisure time between his meetings to accomplish the work.

Out of a large mass of materials before him, the compiler has found it difficult to decide what to *omit*, and what to *retain*, to compose so small a volume.

He has aimed to select the *best*, and generally the *shortest*, of our standard Hymns, introducing a few that are not found in any of our own selections, and also a few composed by himself, imperfect as they are. At the suggestion of some brethren, he has abridged some of the longer Hymns in common use. The little volume of *Pocket Hymns* is now presented to the children of God containing three hundred and forty-five Hymns, and in its first edition, in a plain dress, and, doubtless, not without its defects, like all human productions. It is thought best to print a few Hymns, of long lines, in smaller type, to save space. It has but one Index to the Hymns, and one to the Subjects; and it was not thought necessary to embrace as wide a range of subjects in this as in the larger works, as such, of course, should be on hand wherever needed.

To his indulgent and charitable brethren and sisters in Christ, far and near, and to all the lovers of our exalted Redeemer, the compiler now dedicates this humble *mite*, in Christian love and affection. And may the smiles of the God of all grace rest upon them and upon it; and when we are done lisping his praises here with stammering tongues, may He bring us to sing in his heavenly kingdom, through Jesus Christ our Redeemer. Amen.

ISAAC N. VANMETER.

MACOMB, ILL.,
July, 1867.

HYMNS.

GOD.

HIS BEING AND ATTRIBUTES.

L. M. *Williams.*

The Unity of God.—Deut., vi. 4.

ETERNAL God! Almighty Cause
Of earth, and seas, and worlds unknown;
All things are subject to thy laws,
All things depend on thee alone.

Thy glorious being singly stands,
Of all within itself possessed,
Controlled by none are thy commands,
Thou from thyself alone art blest.

To Thee alone ourselves we owe;
Let heaven and earth due homage pay;
All other gods we disavow,
Deny their claims, renounce their sway.

Spread thy great name through heathen lands;
Their idol deities dethrone;
Reduce the world to thy command;
And reign, as thou art, God alone.

2   L. M.   *Watts.*

God Supreme and Self-sufficient.

WHAT is our God, or what his name?
Nor men can learn, nor angels teach;
He dwells concealed in radiant flame,
Where neither eyes, nor thoughts can reach.

2 The spacious worlds of heavenly light,
Compared with him, how short they fall!
They are too dark, and he too bright;
Nothing are they, and God is all.

3 He spoke the wondrous word, and lo!
Creation rose at his command;
Whirlwinds and seas their limits know,
Bound in the hollow of his hand.

4 There rests the earth, there roll the spheres,
There nature leans, and feels her prop;
But his own self-sufficience bears
The weight of his own glories up.

5 The tide of creatures ebbs and flows,
Measuring their changes by the moon:
No ebb his sea of glory knows;
His age is one eternal noon.

6 Then fly, my song, an endless round,
The lofty tune let Gabriel raise;
All nature dwell upon the sound,
But we can ne'er fulfil the praise.

3   L. M.   *Williams' Col.*

God Self-existent and Immutable.

ALL-POWERFUL, Self-existent God,
  Who all creation dost sustain;
Thou wast, and art, and art to come,
  And everlasting is thy reign.

2 Fixed and eternal as thy days,
    Each glorious attribute divine
  Through ages infinite shall still
    With undiminished lustre shine.

3 Fountain of being! source of good!
    Immutable dost thou remain;
  Nor can the shadow of a change
    Obscure the glories of thy reign.

4 Earth may with all her powers dissolve,
    If such the great Creator's will;
  But thou forever art the same—
    "I AM" is thy memorial still.

4   L. M.   *Watts.*

Omniscience of God.

IN all my vast concerns with thee,
  In vain my soul would try
To shun thy presence, Lord, or flee
  The notice of thine eye.

2 Thy all-surrounding sight surveys
    My rising and my rest;

My public walks, my private ways,
  And secrets of my breast.

3 My thoughts lie open to the Lord
  Before they're formed within;
And ere my lips pronounce the word
  He knows the sense I mean.

4 Oh, wondrous knowledge! deep and high,
  Where can a creature hide?
Within thy circling arms I lie,
  Enclosed on every side.

5 So let thy grace surround me still,
  And like a bulwark prove,
To guard my soul from every ill,
  Secured by sovereign love.

C. M.   *Watts.*

Divine Sovereignty.

KEEP silence, all created things,
  And wait your Maker's nod;
My soul stands trembling while she sings
  The honors of her God.

2 Life, death, and hell, and worlds unknown,
  Hang on his firm decree:
He sits on no precarious throne,
  Nor borrows leave *to be.*

3 Chained to his throne, a volume lies,
   With all the fates of men,
With every angel's form and size,
   Drawn by the eternal pen.

4 His providence unfolds the book,
   And makes his council shine;
Each opening leaf and every stroke
   Fulfills some deep design.

5 Here he exalts neglected worms
   To sceptres and a crown;
And there the following page he turns,
   And treads the monarch down.

6 Not Gabriel asks the reason why,
   Nor God the reason gives;
Nor dares the favorite angel pry
   Between the folded leaves.

7 My God, I would not long to see
   My fate with curious eyes,
What gloomy lines are writ for me,
   Or what bright scenes may rise.

8 In thy fair book of life and grace,
   Oh, may I find my name,
Recorded in some humble place,
   Beneath my Lord the Lamb!

6   S. M.   *Vanmeter*

The Fool. Ps. 14. 1.

THE fool with impudence,
  Saith that "There is no God:
The whole creation came by chance—
  The earth, the skies, the flood.

2 "By chance the sun arose,
  And shone upon the earth.
Chance caused the whistling wind that blows,
  And gave the planets birth."

3 Vain man! if these things came
  By chance, that thou canst see,
How many more things might we name?
  How many might there be?

4 *Might* there not be a GOD?
  Might there not be a hell?
May it not be the dire abode,
  Where thou shalt ever dwell?

7   S. M.   *Watts.*

Omniscience.

LORD, thou hast searched and seen me thro'
  Thine eye commands with piercing view
My rising and my resting hours,
My heart and flesh with all their powers.

2 My thoughts, before they are my own,
  Are to my God distinctly known;

He knows the words I mean to speak
Ere from my opening lips they break.

3 Within thy circling power I stand;
On every side I find thy hand;
Awake, asleep, at home, abroad,
I am surrounded still with God.

4 Amazing knowledge, vast and great!
What large extent! what lofty height!
My soul, with all the powers I boast,
Is in the boundless prospect lost.

5 Oh, may these thoughts possess my breast,
Where'er I rove, where'er I rest!
Nor let my weaker passions dare
Consent to sin, for God is there.

8   C. M.   *Christian Psalmist.*

THERE'S not a tint that paints the rose,
   Or decks the lily fair,
Or streaks the humblest flower that grows,
   But heaven has placed it there.

2 There's not of grass a single blade,
   Or leaf of lowliest mien,
Where heavenly skill is not displayed,
   And heavenly wisdom seen.

3 There's not a star whose twinkling light
    Illumes the distant earth,
And cheers the solemn gloom of night,
    But heaven gave it birth.

4 There's not a place in earth's vast round,
    In ocean's deep, or air,
Where skill and wisdom are not found,—
    For God is everywhere.

9   L. M.   *Addison.*
The Glory of God displayed in the Firmament.

THE spacious firmament on high,
    With all the blue ethereal sky,
And spangled heavens, a shining frame,
Their great Original proclaim.

2 The unwearied sun, from day to day,
Does his Creator's power display,
And publishes to every land
The work of an Almighty hand.

3 Soon as the evening shades prevail,
The moon takes up the wondrous tale;
And nightly to the listening earth
Repeats the story of her birth;

4 While all the stars that round her burn,
And all the planets in their turn,
Confirm the tidings as they roll,
And spread the truth from pole to pole.

5 What though in solemn silence all
  Move round this dark terrestrial ball;
  What though no real voice nor sound
  Amidst their radiant orbs be found;

6 In reason's ear they all rejoice,
  And utter forth a glorious voice,
  Forever singing, as they shine,
  "The hand that made us is divine."

10   C. M.   *Presbyterian Selection.*
God Celebrated in his Works.

I SING the almighty power of God,
  That made the mountains rise,
That spread the flowing seas abroad
  And built the lofty skies.

2 I sing the wisdom that ordained
  The sun to rule the day;
The moon shines full at his command,
  And all the stars obey.

3 I sing the goodness of the Lord,
  That filled the earth with food;
He formed the creatures with his word,
  And then pronounced them good.

4 Lord, how thy wonders are displayed,
  Where'er I turn mine eye!
If I survey the ground I tread,
  Or gaze upon the sky.

5 There's not a plant or flower below,
　　But makes thy glories known;
　And clouds arise and tempests blow
　　By order from thy throne.

6 Creatures, as numerous as they be,
　　Are subject to thy care;
　There's not a place where we can flee,
　　But God is present there.

11　　　　　S. M.　　　　　*Vanmeter.*
The Omnipresence of God.

O SPIRIT, guide my pen;
　　Illuminate my mind;
Help me to spread Jehovah's name
　　Abroad to all mankind.

2 Enthroned above the skies,
　　He dwells in radiant light;
　Beyond the reach of mortal eyes,
　　And clothed in glories bright.

3 But still his works declare,
　　His awful name abroad;
　Yes, every planet, every star,
　　Declares there is a God.

4 'Twas he that formed the sun,
　　By day to give us light;
　'Twas he that said: "Thou silver moon,
　　Illume the shades of night."

5 Yea, every wind that blows,
    And every cloud that flies,
And every spear of grass that grows,
    Presents Him to our eyes.

6 In all creation's frame,
    No new event can rise;
His vast concerns all lie before
    His scrutinizing eyes.

7 Then let all nations stand,
    In awe before His throne;
They rise or fall at His command—
    Beside him there is none.

12   C. M.   *Watts.*

The Mysteries of Providence.

GOD moves in a mysterious way
    His wonders to perform;
He plants his footsteps in the sea,
    And rides upon the storm.

2 Deep in unfathomable mines
    Of never-failing skill,
He treasures up his bright designs,
    And works his sovereign will.

3 Ye fearful saints, fresh courage take;
    The clouds ye so much dread
Are big with mercy, and shall break
    In blessings on your head.

4 Judge not the Lord by feeble sense,
   But trust him for his grace;
Behind a frowning providence
   He hides a smiling face.

5 His purposes will ripen fast,
   Unfolding every hour;
The bud may have a bitter taste,
   But sweet will be the flower.

6 Blind unbelief is sure to err,
   And scan his work in vain;
God is his own interpreter,
   And he will make it plain.

13 L. M. *Vanmeter.*
The Wisdom and Power of God.

WITH what unbounded power and skill,
   Jehovah doth his work perform?
He rules the nations at his will;
   Commands the seas and guides the storm!

2 Now, he exerts creative power;
   Calls forth the earth and worlds unknown;
And then turns realms and kingdoms o'er,
   That dare rebel against his throne.

3 By power, divine, he formed the sun—
   Prodigious fire! amazing light!
'Twas he that formed the silver moon
   To cheer the gloomy shades of night.

4 Ten thousand stars, at his command,
    And planets, roll along the skies;
Sustained by his almighty hand,
    Each, in its orbit, as it flies.

5 His wisdom, like a boundless sea,
    Fixed all his works ere time began:
Naught can disturb his high decree,
    Nor change a feature of his plan.

6 He hath appointed bounds to all
    The tribes and nations of mankind;
Their time to rise, their time to fall,
    Were fixed in his eternal mind.

14   L. M.   *Beddome.*

The Wisdom of God.

WAIT, O my soul, thy maker's will;
    Tumultuous passions, all be still!
Nor let a murmuring thought arise;
His ways are just, his counsels wise.

2 He in the thickest darkness dwells,
Performs his work, the cause conceals;
But, though his methods are unknown,
Judgment and truth support his throne.

3 In heaven, and earth, and air, and seas,
He executes his firm decrees;
And by his saints it stands confessed
That what he does is ever best.

4 Wait then, my soul, submissive wait,
  Prostrate before his awful seat;
  And 'midst the terrors of his rod,
  Trust in a wise and gracious God.

15   L. M.   *Watts.*
            God Invisible.

LORD, we are blind, we mortals blind,
  We can't behold thy bright abode;
O 'tis beyond a creature's mind
To glance a thought half way to God.

2 Infinite leagues beyond the sky
  The Great Eternal reigns alone,
  Where neither wings nor souls can fly,
  Nor angels climb the topless throne.

3 The Lord of Glory builds his seat
  Of gems incomparably bright,
  And lays beneath his sacred feet
  Substantial beams of gloomy night.

4 Yet, glorious Lord, thy gracious eyes
  Look through, and cheer us from above;
  Beyond our praise thy grandeur flies,
  Yet we adore, and yet we love.

16   L. M.   *Watts.*
            The Same.

CAN creatures to perfection find*
  Th' eternal, uncreated mind?

---
*Job xi. 7.

HIS BEING AND ATTRIBUTES. 15

    Or can the largest stretch of thought
    Measure and search his nature out?

2 'Tis high as heaven, 'tis deep as hell,
    And what can mortals know or tell?
    His glory spreads beyond the sky
    And all the shining worlds on high.

3 But man, vain man, would fain be wise;
    Born like a wild young colt he flies
    Through all the follies of his mind,
    And smells, and snuffs the empty wind.

4 God is a King of power unknown,
    Firm are the orders of his throne;
    If he resolves, who dare oppose,
    Or ask him why, or what he does?

5 He wounds the heart and he makes whole;
    He calms the tempest of the soul;
    When he shuts up in long despair,
    Who can remove the heavy bar.

6 *He frowns, and darkness veils the moon
    The fainting sun grows dim at noon;
    †The pillars of heaven's starry roof
    Tremble and start at his reproof.

7 He gave the vaulted heaven its form,
    The crooked serpent and the worm;
    He breaks the billow with his breath,
    And smites the sons of pride to death.

---
*Job xxv. 5. †Job xxvi. 11., &c.

8 These are a portion of his ways,
  And who shall dare describe his face?
  Who can endure his light? or stand
  To hear the thunders of his hand?

17   C. M.   *Fawcett.*
Darkness of Providence.—1 Cor. xiii. 9.

THY way, O God, is in the sea,
  Thy paths I cannot trace;
Nor comprehend the mystery
  Of thy unbounded grace.

2 Here the dark veils of flesh and sense
    My captive soul surround;
  Mysterious deeps of providence
    My wandering thoughts confound.

3 When I behold thy awful hand
    My earthly hopes destroy;
  In deep astonishment I stand,
    And ask the reason why.

4 As through a glass, I dimly see
    The wonders of thy love;
  How little do I know of thee,
    Or of the joys above!

5 'Tis but in part I know thy will;
    I bless thee for the sight:
  When will thy love the rest reveal
    In glory's clearer light?

6 With rapture shall I then survey
  Thy providence and grace:
And spend an everlasting day
  In wonder, love, and praise.

18   L. M.   *Watts.*
      The Darkness of Providence.

LORD, we adore thy vast designs,
  The obscure abyss of providence,
Too deep to sound with mortal lines,
  Too dark to view with feeble sense.

2 Now thou arrayest thine awful face
    In angry frowns, without a smile;
  We through the clouds believe thy grace,
    Secure of thy compassion still.

3 Through seas and storms of deep distress
    We sail by faith and not by sight;
  Faith guides us in the wilderness
    Through all the terrors of the night.

4 Dear Father, if thy lifted rod
    Resolve to scourge us here below,
  Still let us lean upon our God:
    Thine arm shall bear us safely through.

19   .   L. M.   *Vanmeter.*
      God Sovereign, but Man Irreconciled.

WHY should the Lord's divine decrees,
  His sovereign and electing grace,

The sons of men so much displease,
  Or so offend the human race?

2 Although they purpose and ordain
   The works which their own hands perform;
 Yet, they still murmur and complain
   Of Him, who rides upon the storm!

3 Oh! how irreconciled to God,
   Are men in nature and in sin!
 Unwilling that His sovereign nod
   Should rule the world and all within.

4 By his almighty word and will,
   The worlds were framed and made to stand;
 In all their spheres, the planets wheel
   Their endless rounds at his command.

5 In heaven above, and earth, and seas,
   His scepter sways, his words control;
 In all His providence and grace,
   He reigns supreme, from pole to pole.

20   L. M.   *Needham.*
Wisdom and Knowledge of God.—Job xii. 13.

1 AWAKE, my tongue, thy tribute bring
   To Him who gave thee power to sing;
 Praise Him who is all praise above,
 The source of wisdom and of love.

2 How vast his knowledge! how profound!
A depth where all our thoughts are drowned!
The stars he numbers, and their names
He gives to all these heavenly flames.

3 Through each bright world above, behold
Ten thousand thousand charms unfold;
Earth, air, and mighty seas combine
To speak his wisdom all divine.

4 But in redemption, oh, what grace!
To save the sons of Adam's race;
Here wisdom shines forever bright:
Praise him my soul, with sweet delight.

21   S. M.   *Watts.*
God's Awful Power and Goodness.

1 O THE almighty Lord!
   How matchless is his power!
Tremble, O earth, beneath his word,
   While all the heavens adore.

2 Let proud imperious kings
   Bow low before his throne;
Crouch to his feet, ye haughty things,
   Or he shall tread you down.

3 Above the skies he reigns,
   And with amazing blows
He deals unsufferable pains
   On his rebellious foes.

4 Yet, everlasting God,
    We love to speak thy praise;
  Thy scepter's equal to thy rod,
    The scepter of thy grace.

5 The arms of mighty love
    Defend our Zion well,
  And heavenly mercy walls us round
    From Babylon and Hell.

6 Salvation to the King
    That sits enthroned above;
  Thus we adore the God of might,
    And bless the God of love.

22   C. M.   *Watts.*
Sincerity and Hypocrisy; or, Formality in Worship. John iv. 24. Ps. cxxxix. 23, 24.

1 GOD is a Spirit just and wise,
    He sees our inmost mind;
  In vain to heaven we raise our cries,
    And leave our souls behind.

2 Nothing but truth before his throne
    With honor can appear,
  The painted hypocrites are known
    Through the disguise they wear.

3 Their lifted eyes salute the skies,
    Their bending knees the ground;

But God abhors the sacrifice
  Where not the heart is found.

4 Lord, search my thoughts, and try my ways,
    And make my soul sincere;
  Then shall I stand before thy face,
    And find acceptance there.

23   L. M.   *Watts.*

BEFORE Jehovah's awful throne,
  Ye nations, bow with sacred joy;
Know that the Lord is God alone;
  He can create, and he destroy.

2 Ere rolling worlds began to move,
    Or ere the heavens were spread abroad,
  Thy awful throne was fixed above;
    From everlasting thou art God.

3 His sovereign power, without our aid,
    Made us of clay, and formed us men;
  And when like wandering sheep we strayed,
    He brought us to his fold again.

4 [We are his people, we his care,
    Our souls, and all our mortal frame:
  What lasting honors shall we rear,
    Almighty Maker, to thy name?]

5 We'll crowd thy gates with thankful songs,
 High as the heavens our voices raise;
And earth, with her ten thousand tongues,
 Shall fill thy courts with sounding praise.

6 Wide as the world is thy command!
 Vast as eternity thy love!
Firm as a rock thy truth must stand,
 When rolling years shall cease to move.

24   L. M.   *Parkinson's Selection.*
Mysteries.

LORD, how mysterious are thy ways!
 How blind we are! how mean our praise!
Thy steps no mortal can explore;
'Tis ours to wonder and adore!

2 Thy deep decrees, from creature sight,
Are hid in shades of awful night;
Amid the lines, with curious eye,
Not angel minds presume to pry.

3 Great God, I would not ask to see
What in futurity shall be;
If light and bliss attend my days,
Then let my future hours be praise.

4 Is darkness and distress my share?
Then let me trust thy guardian care;
Assured I am that love divine
At length through every cloud will shine.

5 Yet this my soul desires to know,
 Be this my only wish below:
 "That Christ is mine!"—This great request
 Grant, bounteous God! and I am blest!

25   8. 8. 6.   *Mercer's Selection.*
Wonderful Love of God.

WERE oceans, rivers, floods and lakes,
    All that the name water takes,
      Beneath the expanded skies,
 Turned into ink of blackest hue,
 And all the drops of fallen dew,
      To make the wonder rise;

2 Were there a book, could we suppose,
 Which thinnest paper could compose,
      Large as this earthly ball;
 Were every shrub and every tree,
 And every blade of grass we see,
      A pen to write withal;

3 Were all who ever lived on earth,
 Since nature first received her birth,
      The aptest scribes declared,
 To explain the fulness of that *love*
 Found in the heart of God above,
      To men by sin ensnared;

4 Were each *Methuselah* in age,
 And every moment wrote a page,
      They'd all be tired and die:

The pens would every one wear out,
The book be filled within, without,
   The ink would all run dry.

5 And then to show that love, oh, then,
Angels above as well as men,
   Archangels e'en would fail;
Nay, till eternity shall end,
A whole eternity they'll spend,
   Nor then have told the tale.

THE FALL.

26 C. M. *Watts.*
Corrupt Nature from Adam.

BLESSED with the joys of innocence,
   Adam, our father, stood,
'Till he debased his soul to sense,
   And ate the unlawful food.

2 Now we are born a sensual race,
   To sinful joys inclined;
Reason has lost its native place,
   And flesh enslaves the mind.

3 While flesh and sense and passion reign,
   Sin is the sweetest good:

We fancy music in our chain,
   And so forget the load.

4 Eternal Spirit, write thy law
   Upon our inward parts,
And let the second Adam draw
   His image on our hearts.

27   L. M.   *Watts.*

Original Sin.

ADAM, our father and our head,
Transgressed, and justice doomed us dead;
The fiery law speaks all despair,
There's no reprieve nor pardon there.

2 Call a bright council in the skies:
Seraphs, the mighty and the wise,
Speak; are you strong to bear the load,
The weighty vengeance of a God?

3 In vain we ask; for all around
Stand silent through the heavenly ground;
There's not a glorious mind above,
Has half the strength or half the love.

4 But, oh, unmeasurable grace!
God's only Son takes Adam's place;
Down to our world the Saviour flies.
Stretches his arms. and bleeds and dies!

5 Amazing work! look down, ye skies,
Wonder and gaze with all your eyes;
Ye saints below and saints above,
All bow to this mysterious love.

28 C. M. *Dobell's Selec*
Man's Fall and Recovery.—2 Sam. xiv. 14;
1 Cor. xv. 49.

IN Adam's loins, by sin we fell,
And walked destruction's road,
Without a will or power to turn
To happiness and God.

2 But God ordained the way to bring
His banished children home;
And Christ fulfilled the wondrous plan
By his own death alone.

3 The Spirit brings his exiles back
As trophies of his love,
And plants within them holy fear,
No more from God to rove.

4 [Ye saints, proclaim Jehovah's praise,
And shout his honors high:
His grace shall be your lasting theme,
When time itself shall die.]

29 L. M. *Watts*
The first and second Adam.—Rom. v. 12.

DEEP in the dust before thy throne,
Our guilt and our disgrace we own;

Great God! we own the unhappy name
Whence sprung our nature and our shame,—

2 Adam, the sinner: at his fall,
Death, like a conquerer, seized us all;
A thousand new-born babes are dead
By fatal union to their head.

3 But whilst our spirits, filled with awe,
Behold the terrors of thy law,
We sing the honors of thy grace,
That sent to save our ruined race.

4 We sing thine everlasting Son,
Who joined our nature to his own;
The second Adam, from the dust,
Raises the ruins of the first.

5 [By the rebellion of *one* man,
Through all *his* seed the mischief ran,
And by *one* man's obedience now
Are all *his* seed made righteous too.]

6 Where sin did reign, and death abound,
There have the sons of Adam found
Abounding life; there glorious grace
Reigns through the Lord our righteousness.

30 C. M. *Watts.*
Original Sin; or, the first and second Adam.—
Rom. v. 12; Psa. ii. 5; Job xiv. 4.

BACKWARD with humble shame we look
On our original:

How is our nature dashed and broke
  In our first father's fall!

2 To all that's good averse and blind,
    But prone to all that's ill;
  What dreadful darkness veils our mind!
    How obstinate our will!

3 [Conceived in sin, (oh, wretched state!)
    Before we draw our breath,
  The first young pulse begins to beat
    Iniquity and death.

4 How strong in our degenerate blood
    The old corruption reigns,
  And, mingling with the crooked flood,
    Wanders through all our veins!]

5 [Wild and unwholesome as the root
    Will all the branches be:
  How can we hope for living fruit
    From such a deadly tree?

6 What mortal power, from things unclean,
    Can pure productions bring?
  Who can command a vital stream
    From an infected spring?]

7 Yet, mighty God, thy wondrous love
    Can make our nature clean,
  While Christ and grace prevail above
    The tempter, death, and sin.

8 The second Adam shall restore
   The ruins of the first;
Hosanna to that sovereign power
   That new-creates our dust.

31 L. M. *Vanmeter.*
Man's Fall and Recovery.

OH! painful truth, it is to tell,
   That Adam, our first father, fell,
And brought upon his unborn race,
Eternal misery and disgrace.

2 The law arose in mighty wrath,
   And passed the sentence of our death;
The sword of justice then awoke
And raised o'er us its dreadful stroke.

3 Hold! hold! forgiving mercy cries!
   For sin there is a sacrifice:
Behold! the gracious Son of God
Agrees to bear the heavy load!

4 Down from the realms of endless day,
   With speed the Saviour makes his way;
Fulfills the law, pours out his blood,
To bring his people back to God.

5 O! let the world, with all its dross,
   Withdraw, that I may view the cross!
'Tis there I lean and take repose,
And thence my greatest comfort flows.

32   C. M.   *Watts*
Fatal Depravity.

SIN, like a venomous disease,
  Infects our vital blood;
The only balm is sovereign grace,
  And the physician, God.

2 Our beauty and our strength are fled,
  And we draw near to death;
But Christ the Lord recalls the dead
  With his almighty breath.

3 Madness by nature reigns within,
  The passions burn and rage;
Till God's own Son, with skill divine,
  The inward fire assuage.

4 [We lick the dust, we grasp the wind,
  And solid good despise:
Such is the folly of the mind
  Till Jesus makes us wise.

5 We give our souls the wounds they feel,
  We drink the poisonous gall,
And rush with fury down to hell;
  But heaven prevents the fall.]

6 [The man possessed among the tombs
  Cuts his own flesh, and cries;
He foams and raves till Jesus comes,
  And the foul spirit flies.]

33   L. M.   *Vanmeter.*
The Effects of Sin.

SIN is the only evil thing
   That we on earth are subject to;
It gives to death its greatest sting,
   And leads to misery and woe.

2 Sin hurled our parents from their bliss,
   And ruined all their progeny;
Destroyed their happiness and peace,
   And made the earth a curse to be.

3 Yea, all the noble powers of man,
   Were thus polluted by its stain;
Through all his soul the poison ran,
   Through all his life he suffers pain.

4 Sin dwells upon the sinner's tongue,
   And reigns and rules within his heart;
And as she makes her fetters strong,
   Seizes and holds on every part.

5 No earthly power nor human skill,
   Can wash away the dreadful stain:
To cleanse the heart, renew the will,
   Their works and efforts all are vain.

6 Nothing but Christ's atoning blood
   Can wash the hateful stain away;
And bring the sinner back to God,
   And fit him for eternal day.

34   C. M.   *Vanmeter.*

The Nature and Effects of Transgression.

WHEN man transgressed the law of God,
    He ruined all his race ;
The raging poison spread abroad,
    And plunged us in disgrace.

2 Wretch, that he was, to thus rebel
    And prostrate all his seed !
'Twas Satan, the foul fiend of hell,
    The dreadful project laid.

3 First, he made known his hellish plot,
    And man imbibed the sin ;
The eating was but acting out
    The principle within.

4 Oh, horrid crime ! what mischief hung
    Around that dreadful hour !
Thence death and all the miseries sprung,
    That spread creation o'er !

5 God's justice claimed the sinner's blood,
    His wrath was now revealed ;
And all the attributes of God
    His condemnation sealed.

6 By the offense of the first man
    Our condemnation came :
If poison at the fount began,
    The streams partake the same.

THE FALL.

C. M. — Vanmeter.

The Effects of Sin and the Reign of Grace.

OUR father lost his innocence,
  Incurred the frowns of heaven;
From Eden's flowery garden, thence,
  By justice he was driven.

2 The seeds of sin put forth their roots
  Through all the human heart;
And all creation felt the fruits
  Corruption did impart.

3 While justice guards, with jealous eyes,
  The spotless throne of God,
No guilty rebel can arise
  And dwell in his abode.

4 But Jesus is the glorious head
  Of all his chosen seed;
In Adam we behold them dead,
  In Christ we see them freed.

5 The flaming sword of justice wakes
  Against the Lamb of God;
And Christ for his own body makes
  Atonement by his blood.

6 In Adam we transgressed the law,
  In Christ we kept the same;
And his own robe of righteousness,
  Our glorious robe became.

L. M. *Watts.*
Custom of Sin.

LET the wild leopards of the wood
 Put off the spots that nature gives,
Then may the wicked turn to God,
 And change their tempers and their lives.

2 As well might Ethiopian slaves
 Wash out the darkness of their skin,
The dead as well may leave their graves
 As old transgressors cease to sin.

3 Where vice has held its empire long,
 'Twill not endure the least control;
None but a power divinely strong
 Can turn the current of the soul.

4 Great God, I own thy power divine,
 That works to change this heart of mine;
I would be formed anew, and bless
 The wonders of creating grace.

THE SCRIPTURES.

37   7s.   2 *Tim.* 111, 16.
The Scripture is an Instructor and Monitor to the Christian.

HOLY Bible! book divine!
Precious treasure! thou art mine!
Mine to teach me whence I came—
Mine to teach me what I am:

2 Mine to chide me when I rove—
Mine to show a Savior's love—
Mine art thou to guard my feet—
Mine to judge, condemn, acquit:

3 Mine to comfort in distress,
If the Holy Spirit bless—
Mine, to show by living faith,
Man can triumph over death:

4 Mine to tell of joys to come,
And the rebel sinner's doom;
O thou precious book divine!
Precious treasure! thou art mine!

38   8. 7.   *Newton.*
The Scriptures a Support to the Christian.

PRECIOUS Bible! what a treasure
Does the word of God afford!

All I want for life, for pleasure,
  Food and medicine, shield and sword ;
    Let the world account me poor—
    Having this, I want no more.

2 Food to which the world's a stranger,
    Here my hungry soul enjoys ;
  Of excess there is no danger—
    Though it fills, it never cloys :
      On a dying Christ I feed—
      He is meat and drink indeed.

3 When my faith is faint and sickly
    Or when Satan wounds my mind,
  Cordials to revive me quickly,
    Healing medicines here I find ;
      To the promises I flee—
      Each affords a remedy.

4 In the hour of dark temptation,
    Satan cannot make me yield ;
  For the word of consolation
    Is to me a mighty shield ;
      While the scripture truths are sure,
      From his malice I'm secure.

5 Vain his threats to overcome me,
    When I take the Spirit's sword ;
  Then with ease I drive him from me—
    Satan trembles at the word ;
      'Tis a sword of conquest made—
      Keen the edge and strong the blade.

6 Shall I envy then the miser,
　　Doating on his golden store?
　Sure I am, or should be wiser,
　　I am rich—'tis he is poor:
　　　Jesus gives me in his word,
　　　Food and medicine, shield and sword.

39　　　　C. M.　　　　*Watts.*
The Inspired Word, a System of Knowledge and Joy. Psalms, cxix. 105.

HOW precious is the book divine,
　　By inspiration given!
Bright as a lamp its doctrines shine
　　To guide our souls to heaven.

2 It sweetly cheers our drooping hearts
　　In this dark vale of tears;
Life, light and joy it still imparts,
　　And quells our rising fears.

3 This lamp, through all the tedious night
　　Of life, shall guide our way;
Till we behold the clearer light
　　Of an eternal day.

40　　　　C. M.　　　　*Mrs. Steele.*
The Excellence and Sufficiency of the Holy Scriptures.

FATHER of mercies! in thy word
　　What endless glory shines!

Forever be thy name adored
　　　For these celestial lines.

2 Here, may the wretched sons of want
　　　Exhaustless riches find;
　Riches above what earth can grant,
　　　And lasting as the mind.

3 Here, the fair tree of knowledge grows,
　　　And yields a free repast;
　Sublimer sweets than nature knows
　　　Invite the longing taste.

4 Here the Redeemer's welcome voice
　　　Spreads heavenly peace around;
　And life, and everlasting joys,
　　　Attend the blissful sound.

5 O may these heavenly pages be
　　　My ever dear delight;
　And still new beauties may I see,
　　　And still increasing light!

6 Divine Instructor, gracious Lord!
　　　Be thou for ever near;
　Teach me to love thy sacred word,
　　　And view my Savior there!

41　　　　　L. M.　　　　　*Watts.*
　　　　Prophesy and Inspiration.

'TWAS by an order from the Lord,
　　The ancient prophets spoke his word;

His Spirit did their tongues inspire,
And warmed their hearts with heavenly fire.

2 The works and wonders which they wrought
Confirmed the messages they brought;
The prophet's pen succeeds his breath
To save the holy words from death.

3 Great God, mine eyes with pleasure look
On the dear volume of thy book;
There my Redeemer's face I see,
And read his name who died for me.

4 Let the false raptures of the mind
Be lost and vanish in the wind;
Here I can fix my hopes secure,
This is thy word, and must endure.

42   C. M. *Christian Psalmist.*

GREAT God, with wonder and with praise
On all thy works I look;
But still thy wisdom, power and grace,
Shine brightest in thy book.

2 Here are my choicest treasures hid,
Here my best comfort lies;
Here my desires are satisfied,
And here my hopes arise.

3 Lord, make me understand thy law;
Show what my faults have been;

And from thy gospel let me draw
　　The pardon of my sin.

43　　　　　　　C. M.　　　　　　　*Watts.*
The Holy Scriptures.

LADEN with guilt, and full of fears,
　　I fly to thee, my Lord;
And not a glimpse of hope appears
　　But in thy written word.

2 The volume of my Father's grace
　　Does all my griefs assuage;
Here I behold my Savior's face
　　Almost in every page.

3 This is the field where hidden lies
　　The pearl of price unknown;
That merchant is divinely wise
　　Who makes the pearl his own.

4 Here consecrated water flows
　　To quench my thirst of sin;
Here the fair tree of knowledge grows,
　　Nor danger dwells within.

5 This is the judge that ends the strife,
　　Where wit and reason fail;
My guide to everlasting life
　　Through all this gloomy vale.

6 Oh, may thy counsels, mighty God,
　My roving feet command;
Nor I forsake the happy road
　That leads to thy right hand.

44　　　　　　8. 8. 6.　　　　　*Sonnets.*
The Letter Killeth, but the Spirit Giveth Life.

WHAT if we read and understand
　The written word of God's command,
　　And give it credit meet;
The word is but a looking-glass,
And only shows a man his face,
　　Unless the word we eat.

2 It raiseth no man from the dead,
While seated only in the head,
　　But leaves him dry and faint:
It maketh matter for some talk,
But cannot give him legs to walk,
　　Nor make a man a saint.

3 The word consists of letters fair,
But letters merely dead things are,
　　And cannot change the heart;
The letter only bringeth death,
Unless the Spirit by his breath
　　A quickening power impart.

4 May thy commands obedience get,
And promises yield comforts sweet

And threatenings awe my soul;
Let exhortations spur me on,
And cautions make me watchful run,
And love inspire the whole.

5 According as my wants require,
Adapt the word as food and fire,
To nourish and to warm;
Let every page afford new wealth,
Convey some life and godly health,
And guard my steps from harm.

THE LAW.

45   L. M.   *Watts.*
The Law and Gospel Distinguished.

THE law commands, and makes us know
What duties to our God we owe;
But 'tis the gospel must reveal
Where lies our strength to do his will.

2 The law discovers guilt and sin,
And shows how vile our hearts have been;
Only the gospel can express
Forgiving love and cleansing grace.

3 What curses doth the law denounce
Against the man that fails but once!

> But in the gospel Christ appears
> Pardoning the guilt of numerous years.

4 My soul, no more attempt to draw
Thy life and comfort from the law,
Fly to the hope the gospel gives;
The man that trusts the promise lives.

46   S. M.   *Watts.*
The Law and Gospel.

THE Lord declares his will,
    And keeps the world in awe;
Amidst the smoke on Sinai's hill
    Breaks out his fiery law.

2 The Lord reveals his face,
    And smiling from above,
Sends down the gospel of his grace,
    The epistles of his love.

3 These sacred words impart
    Our Maker's just commands;
The pity of his melting heart,
    And vengeance of his hands.

4 [Hence we awake our fear,
    We draw our comfort hence;
The arms of grace are treasured here,
    And armor of defence.

5 We learn Christ crucified,
    And here behold his blood;

All arts and knowledges beside
  Will do us little good.]

6 We read the heavenly word,
  The record of his grace,
Obey the statutes of the Lord,
  And trust his promises.

7 In vain shall Satan rage
  Against a book divine;
Where wrath and lightning guard the page,
Where beams of mercy shine.

47 L. M. *Watts.*
The Practical Use of the Law to the Convinced Sinner.

HERE, Lord, my soul convicted stands
  Of breaking all thy ten commands;
And on me justly mightst thou pour
Thy wrath in one eternal shower.

2 But, thanks to God! its loud alarms
  Have warned me of approaching harms;
And now, O Lord, my wants I see;
Lost and undone I come to thee.

3 I see my fig-leaf righteousness
  Can ne'er thy broken law redress;
Yet, in thy gospel plan, I see
There's hope of pardon e'en for me.

4 Here I behold thy wonders, Lord!
　How Christ hath to thy law restored
　Those honors, on the atoning day,
　Which guilty sinners took away.

5 Amazing wisdom, power and love,
　Displayed to rebels from above!
　Do thou, O Lord, my faith increase,
　To love and trust thy plan of grace.

48   L. M.   *Vanmeter.*
The Law and the Gospel.

THE law and gospel both agree
　In glorifying Deity;
And yet a difference we must draw
Between the gospel and the law.

2 The law exhibits to our view,
　A God that's holy, just and true;
　But 'tis the gospel must express
　How he extends his sovereign grace.

3 The law the guilty wretch condemns,
　And must have all its righteous claims:
　The gospel sets the prisoner free,
　And speaks the voice of liberty.

4 The law convinces us of sin,
　And shows how vile our lives have been:
　The gospel doth a fountain show,
　At once to cleanse and pardon too.

5 The law is holy, just and good,
   And justly claims the sinner's blood:
   The gospel shows that Jesus shed
   His precious blood in sinners' stead.

6 Thus, from Mount Sinai we behold
   The law came forth in days of old;
   But Calvary shows a sacrifice,
   Whence all our hopes and comforts rise.

49   C. M.   *Vanmeter.*

The Insufficiency of a Law Righteousness.

DO not frustrate the grace of God;
   For if our righteousness
Came by the law, then Jesus' blood
   Is null and void of grace.

2 For by the deeds of Moses' law
   No flesh is justified:
We can no hope of comfort draw
   Till Jesus' blood's applied.

3 To him that works, is the reward,
   Not reckoned of free grace;
But faith in Jesus Christ, the Lord,
   Is counted righteousness.

4 Why should the blessed Savior die,
   And shed his precious blood;
If man the law could satisfy
   And make the payment good?

5 Not all the Jews e'er sacrificed
    Could make the conscience clean;
But the atoning blood of Christ,
    Will cleanse from every sin.

6 Wash me, dear Savior, in thy blood,
    And make me white as snow,
Then I will follow thee, my God,
    And will no other know.

50   S. M.   *Songs in the Night.*
The Law is Spiritual.—Rom. vii. 14.

THE law of God is just,
    A strict and holy way;
And he that would escape the curse
    Must all the law obey.

2 Not one vain thought must rise,
    Not one unclean desire;
He must be holy, just, and wise,
    Who keeps the law entire.

3 If in one point he fail,
    In thought, or word, or deed,
The curses of the law prevail,
    And rest upon his head.

4 Now let me bring my heart,
    And with the law compare,
And ask if I in every part
    Have paid obedience there.

5 I tremble and retreat;
  Behold, O God! I'm vile:
 Guilty, I fall before thy feet,
  And own my nature's soil.

6 Lord I've transgressed thy law;
  I now lament my sin;
 Still I offend in all I do,
  I'm carnal and unclean.

7 And does the curse still rest
  Upon my guilty head?
 No: Jesus—let his name be blest!—
  Hath borne it in my stead.

8 He hath fulfilled the law,
  Obtained my peace with God:
 Hence doth my soul her comforts draw,
  And leave her heavy load.

51   8s.   *Kent*

Jesus the End of the Law.

LET those who inhabit the Rock,
  And out of his fulness receive,
Proclaim him the tower of the flock,
  Still precious to them that believe;
Our Prophet, our Priest, and our King,
  'Tis life everlasting to know;
His blood and his merits we sing,
  For Christ is the End of the Law.

2 'Tis here, when with sorrows oppressed,
    Believers in Jesus should flee;
  For those that are weary there's rest,
    For sin-burdened sinners like me;
  If Justice pursues thee for blood,
    His righteousness stands without flaw;
  And he that redeemed thee to God,
    Is Jesus the End of the Law.

3 The types and the shadows are fled,
    With all that prediction foretold;
  Since Jesus on Calvary bled,
    His sheep shall return to the fold;
  Shall build upon him as a Rock,
    Nor fear when the tempest shall blow,
  And nothing the building shall shock,
    For Christ is the End of the Law.

4 How sweet and delightful the strain,
    Salvation by grace to repeat;
  Shall sinners redeemed e'er refrain,
    Who stand as in Jesus complete?
  From him, as the fountain of life,
    His saints their existence shall draw,
  And live, though encompassed with strife,
    For Christ is the End of the Law.

52   C. M.   Kent.
    Law and Gospel.—Phil. iii. 7–10.

WHEN from the precepts to the cross
  The humble sinner turns,

His brightest deeds he counts but dross,
  And o'er his vileness mourns.

2 God, on the table of his heart,
    Inscribes his love and fear;
  He loves the law in every part,
    But takes no refuge there.

3 Thus gospel, law, and justice too,
    Conspire to set him free:
  Reflect, my soul, admire and view
    What God hath done for thee.

53. L. M. *Kent's Selection.*

Help Laid in Christ.—Psa. lxxxix. 19.

FROM Sinai's mount to Zion's hill,
    Insolvents, haste away;
  The law's demands ye can't fulfill,
    For ye have naught to pay.

2 Then to the cross of Jesus, now,
    Ye guilty souls, repair;
  There justice wears a smiling brow,
    And mercy triumphs there.

3 His work was great: 'twas to redeem,
    And bring to glory all
  The chosen seed, beloved in him,
    Selected from the fall.

4 And who but the Redeemer, say,
　　Was able to endure
　The weight of sin that on him lay,
　　And make salvation sure?

5 Vindictive wrath, to sinners due,
　　His sacred bosom tore;
　And pains, that mortals never knew,
　　Brought blood from every pore.

6 Yet he was able to fulfill
　　Salvation's glorious plan;
　The councils of Jehovah's will,
　　Before the world began.

54　　　　　　C. M.　　　　　　*Kent.*
The Sinner seeking Life by the Works of the Law.

BEHOLD how Adam's helpless race,
　　Are striving, though in vain,
Who think, by works, and not by grace,
　　Salvation to obtain.

2 Though dead in sin, they struggle hard,
　　And seek to enter in
　The gate that flaming cherubs guard,
　　Forever shut by sin.

3 But when the killing law takes place,
　　It makes their efforts null;
　Salvation then appears of grace
　　Abundant, free, and full.

4 Now from the precepts to the cross
 His eyes the sinner turns;
 His brighter deeds he counts but dross,
 And o'er his vileness mourns.

5 God, on the table of his heart,
 Inscribes his love and fear,
 He loves the law in every part,
 But takes no refuge there.

6 Give us, O God, thy grace to see
 The only fountain, thou—
 Then shall we own salvation free,
 And at thy footstool bow.

THE GOSPEL.

55   L. M.   *Col.*

Beginning at Jerusalem.—Luke xxiv. 47.

PROCLAIM my gospel, saith the Lord,
 Ye preachers of my sacred word;
Let every nation hear the theme,
Beginning at Jerusalem.

2 Go; let the chief of sinners know,
 That I have blessings to bestow:
 Proclaim salvation in my name,
 Beginning at Jerusalem.

3 Where I was treated with disdain,
  Where I was crucified and slain,
  There shall my gospel gain esteem,
  Beginning at Jerusalem.

4 My pardoning love proclaim abroad,
  And show the virtue of my blood;
  Till time shall end, proclaim my grace,
  To every land, in every place.

5 In yonder world, behold the train
  Of sinners saved from endless pain,
  Ascribing glory to the Lamb,
  Within the new Jerusalem.

56   C. M.   *Kent.*
Prophesying to the Dry Bones.

WHILE in the vale of vision, dead,
    The house of Israel lie,
  Jehovah to the prophet said,
    Go thou, and prophesy.

2 Go thou, nor reasoning scruples make
    Because the bones are dry;
  My voice shall bid the dead awake:
    Go thou, and prophesy.

3 I'll bid the dying sinner live,
    To lift my name on high;
  Eternal life 'tis mine to give;
    Go thou, and prophesy.

4 Hold Jesus to the sinners' view,
   And thither turn their eye;
'Tis I must give to will and do:
   Go thou, and prophesy.

5 From stones, to celebrate my grace,
   While mercy's tidings fly,
My arm shall raise a numerous race,
   Go thou, and prophesy.

57   L. M.   *Cole.*
The Gospel a Joyful Sound.—Ps. lxxxix. 15.

COME, dearest Lord, who reigns above,
   And draw me with the cords of love!
And while the gospel does abound,
"Oh, may I know the joyful sound!"

2 Sweet are the tidings, free the grace,
It brings to our apostate race;
It spreads its heavenly light around:
"Oh, may I know the joyful sound!"

3 The gospel bids the sin-sick soul
Look up to Jesus and be whole;
In him are peace and pardon found:
"Oh, may I know the joyful sound!"

4 It stems the tide of swelling grief,
Affords the needy sure relief,
Releases those by Satan bound:
"Oh, may I know the joyful sound!"

58   C. M.
The Joyful Sound of the Gospel.

THE glorious gospel of our God
    Is joyful news from heaven;
Salvation free in Jesus' blood,
    And life eternal given.

2 'Tis not the gospel's joyful sound
    That fallen men declare,
When Sinai's thunders they confound
    With Zion's beauties fair.

3 He needs no creature-power or skill
    His finished work to mend;
But works his own eternal will,
    As wisdom did intend.

4 When Uzzah stretched his puny hand,
    Behold his awful fall;
The shaking ark secure shall stand,
    When God designs it shall.

5 If 'tis of works, and not of grace,
    No crown shall mortals have,
For all the good of Adam's race
    A single soul can't save.

6 To God, the Father's, love divine,
    The Spirit and the Son,
Let everlasting honors shine,
    While years eternal run.

THE GOSPEL.

59   L. M.   *Vanmeter.*

The Gospel Herald.

IN your great Master's holy name,
  Go forth, ye heralds, and proclaim
The heavenly news to fallen men,
That Jesus died, but lives again.

2 Tell those who in His temple meet,
  To wait and worship at His feet,
That He delights to meet them there—
That He delights to answer prayer.

3 Tell doubting saints fresh courage take;
  That Jesus never will forsake;
That all His promises shall stand,
Long as He holds divine command.

4 Tell mourning souls to trust His grace,
  That Jesus hath prepared a place
For all the blind, and halt, and lame,
Who hate their sins and fear His name.

5 Yea, publish and proclaim His word,
  'Till all Columbia's shores have heard
Of all the victories He hath won,
And all the wonders He hath done.

6 Nor let His glories be confined
  Short of the limits of mankind;
That every kingdom, clime and place
May hear the gospel of His grace.

60   L. M.   *Watts.*
The Commission.

"GO preach my gospel," saith the Lord—
   "Bid mourning souls my grace receive;
He shall be saved that trusts my word—
   He shall be damned that won't believe.

2 ["I'll make your great commission known
   And ye shall prove my gospel true,
By all the works that I have done—
   By all the wonders ye shall do.]

3 ["Go heal the sick, go raise the dead,
   Go cast out devils in my name;
Nor let my prophets be afraid,
   Tho' Greeks reproach, and Jews blaspheme.

4 "Teach all the nations my commands—
   I'm with you till the world shall end;
All power is trusted in my hands—
   I can destroy, and I defend."

5 He spake, and light shone round his head;
   On a bright cloud to heaven he rode;
They to the furthest nation spread
   The grace of their ascended God.

61   C. M.   *Kent.*
Jesus the Sum and Substance of the Gospel.

JESUS the sum and substance is
   Of all the gospel scheme;

In him salvation, all of grace,
    Shines with refulgent beam.

2 Jehovah's councils and decrees,
    Before the world began,
  With all the gospel promises,
    Respect his only Son.

3 Prophetic lore declared his birth,
    His mission, and his name;
  Ages before to this our earth
    The Friend of sinners came.

4 Favored Isaiah heard him groan,
    Saw Justice smite his head;
  Oppressed with sins, but not his own,
    And to the slaughter led.

5 His one great sacrifice complete
    Hath made his Israel free;
  The Paschal Lamb, by faith, they eat,
    And this deliverance see.

6 His church he purchased with his blood,
    And who shall dare condemn?
  But ne'er removed the wrath of God,
    For God was love to them.

62   S. M.   *Watts*
Gospel Ministers.

HOW beauteous are their feet
    Who stand on Zion's hill!

THE GOSPEL.

   Who bring salvation on their tongues,
      And words of peace reveal!

2 How charming is their voice!
      How sweet the tidings are!
   "Zion, behold thy Savior-King,
      He reins and triumphs here."

3 How happy are our ears
      That hear this joyful sound,
   Which kings and prophets waited for,
      And sought, but never found!

4 How blessed are our eyes
      That see this heavenly light!
   Prophets and kings desired it long,
      But died without the sight.

5 The watchmen join their voice,
      And tuneful notes employ;
   Jerusalem breaks forth in songs,
      And deserts learn the joy.

6 The Lord makes bare his arm
      Through all the earth abroad;
   Let every nation now behold
      Their Savior and their God.

63　　　　　C. M.　　　　　*Watts.*
The Different Success of the Gospel—1 Cor. xxiii, 24.

CHRIST and his cross are all our theme:
   The mysteries that we speak

Are scandal in the Jew's esteem,
  And folly to the Greek.

2 But souls enlightened from above
    With joy receive the word;
  They see what wisdom, power, and love
    Shine in their dying Lord.

3 The vital savor of his name
    Restores their fainting breath;
  But unbelief perverts the same
    To guilt, despair, and death.

4 Till God diffuse his graces down,
    Like showers of heavenly rain,
  In vain Apollos sows the ground,
    And Paul may plant in vain.

64   P. M.   *Abridged.*
The Jubilee.

BLOW ye the trumpet, blow
  The gladly solemn sound!
Let all the nations know,
  To earth's remotest bound,
The year of Jubilee is come;
Return, ye ransomed sinners, home.

2 Exalt the Lamb of God,
    The sin-atoning Lamb;
  Redemption by his blood
    Through all the lands proclaim:

The year of Jubilee is come;
Return, ye ransomed sinners, home.

3 The gospel trumpet hear,
　The news of pardoning grace;
Ye happy souls, draw near,
　Behold your Savior's face:
The year of Jubilee is come;
Return, ye ransomed sinners, home.

4 Jesus, our great High-Priest,
　Has full atonement made;
Ye weary spirits, rest;
　Ye mournful souls, be glad!
The year of Jubilee is come;
Return, ye ransomed sinners, home.

7s. 6s.　　　　　*Vanmeter.*

"Who is sufficient for these things?"—2 Cor., ii, 16.

LORD, who can be sufficient to speak thy wondrous name
　And to the heirs of promise thy gospel to proclaim?
preach, as thy salvation, a Saviour crucified,
I speak of all his counsels, concerning of his bride?

ll we seek worldly wisdom, to fit us for the task?
o to schools of learning, and there instructions ask?
ll we seek filthy lucre, or preach for earthly gain?
trive to please the fancy of vain and carnal men?

l we, for fear of slander, the gospel sacrifice?
ike a base delinquent, conceal one-half the price?
l we permit Assyrians to tread on holy ground,
fail to raise the shepherds* and cause the trump to sound?

ah, v. 5.

Forbid it, O, King Jesus! forbid that we should fly,
But fight with holy weapons, and conquer though we die;
To thee we look for courage, and patience to endure;
For wisdom and instruction, that we may feed the poor.

We ask thy Holy Spirit to give us light divine—
For what is worldly wisdom, compared, O Lord, with thine?
We'll bear the vile reproaches, of Jesus and his word,
And count them greater riches, than Egypt can afford.

Be this our constant study, to be approved of God—
To glorify our Savior and spread his name abroad,
To seek Messiah's kingdom, and trust in him alone,
For all our earthly comforts, and blessings of his throne.

66 L. M. Kent.
The Gospel Chariot.

GREAT Salem's King, of old renowned,
With wisdom blest, and honors crowned,
Prepared a chariot for his bride,
That she in princely state might ride.

2 Behold the silver columns stand,
Fair and magnificently grand;
'Twas paved with love, and all to prove
How much he did this fair one love.

3 Fair type of Jesus, whom we love,
Who sent his chariot from above,
To fetch his church, without a stain,
With him in bliss to live and reign.

4 Thus shall the gospel chariot run
Till the last stage of time is done,
And bear in triumph to their God
The ransomed race, redeemed with blood.

5 Yet none shall in this chariot ride,
  Save his elect, his ransomed bride;
  With him, her Lord, in royal state,
  She'll enter Zion's pearly gate,

6 Then, in a song of sweet accord,
  With blood-bought saints to hymn her Lord,
  In strains more noble, sweet, and strong,
  Than e'er were heard in seraph's song.

87 S. M. *Watts.*
Moses and Christ.—John i, 17. Heb. iii, 3, 5. 6,
  x, 28, 29.

THE law by Moses came,
  But peace and truth, and love
Were brought by Christ—a noble name,
  Descended from above.

2 Amidst the house of God,
    There different works are done;
  Moses, a faithful servant stood,
    But Christ a faithful Son.

3 Then to his new commands
    Be strict obedience paid;
  O'er all his father's house he stands,
    The Sovereign and the Head.

4 The man that dares despise
    The law that Moses brought—

Behold how terribly he dies
For his presumptuous fault.

68   L. M.   *W. Thompson.*
*The Gospel Presents Christ to the renewed Mind
for Comfort.*

THE Savior sent the gospel forth,
From east to west, from south to north,
To nations scattered far and wide,
In lands remote, and ocean's tide.

2 Go tell the world what Christ hath done,
Go preach his righteousness alone—
Go publish all he did and said,
And how he bruised the serpent's head.

3 When ears are given, men will hear—
When hearts to feel, they'll feel and fear
When eyes to see, they'll view the prize
The gospel brings before their eyes.

4 Come, Holy Spirit, life impart—
Come know thyself—renew the heart;
With Gospel seed then sow the ground,
And in our lives let fruit be found.

69   C. M.   *W. Thompson.*
*The Spirit must prepare the Heart to receive the
Gospel.*

THE Holy Spirit must renew,
And give us life divine;

No means or agents are employed—
  The work is wholly thine.

2 The gospel and the written word
    Are gifts the Lord bestows,
  To teach his friends and feed his flock,
    And vanquish all his foes.

3 This weapon is to Zion given,—
    Her watchmen should it use;
  And Anti-Christ its power shall feel—
    The Heathen, Greeks, and Jews.

4 By it the sheep and lambs are fed,
    And every heir is taught;
  It is a light to guide their feet
    Till they're to glory brought.

70   C. M.   *Rippon's Select*
    The Gospel a Feast.—Isa. xxv. 6.

ON Zion, his most holy mount,
  God will a feast prepare,
And Israel's sons and Gentile lands
  Shall in the banquet share.

2 Marrow and fatness are the food
    His bounteous hand bestows;
  Wine on the lees, and well refined,
    In rich abundance flows.

3 See to the vilest of the vile
    A free acceptance given !

See rebels, by adopting grace,
    Sit with the heirs of heaven!

4 The pained, the sick, the dying, now
    To ease and health restored,
With eager appetites partake
    The plenties of the board.

5 But, oh, what draughts of bliss unknown,
    What dainties, shall be given,
When, with the myriads round the throne,
    We join the feast of heaven!

6 There joys immeasurably high
    Shall overflow the soul,
And springs of life that never dry
    In thousand channels roll.

71   11s.   *Hart.*
The Gospel.—1 Tim. i. 15.

THE gospel brings tidings to each wounded soul,
That Jesus, the Savior, can make it quite whole;
And what makes this gospel most precious to me,
It holds forth salvation so perfectly free!

2 The gospel declares that God, sending his Son
To die for poor sinners, gave all things in one;
This, too, makes the gospel most precious to me,
Because 'tis a gospel as full as 'tis free!

3 Since Jesus has saved me, and that freely too,
I fain would in all things my gratitude show;
But as to man's merit, 'tis hateful to me!
The gospel—I love it; 'tis perfectly free!

CHRIST—HIS DIVINITY AND INCARNATION.

72   8s.   *Newton.*

What think ye of Christ?—Matt. xxii. 42.

WHAT think ye of Christ? is the test
   To try both your state and your scheme:
You cannot be right in the rest,
   Unless you think rightly of him.

2 As Jesus appears in your view,
   As he is beloved or not,
So God is disposed to you,
   And mercy or wrath is your lot.

3 Some take him a creature to be,
   A man, or an angel at most:
Sure these have not feelings like me,
   Nor know themselves wretched and lost.

So guilty, so helpless, am I,
   I durst not confide in his blood.

Nor on his protection rely,
  Unless I were sure he was God.

5 If asked what of Jesus I think,
   ('Tho' still my best thoughts are but poor,)
  I say, he's my meat and my drink,
   My life, and my strength, and my store,

6 My Shepherd, my husband, my friend,
   My Savior from sin and from thrall;
  My hope from beginning to end,
   My portion, my Lord, and my all.

73   8s.   *Maxwell.*
Unsearchable Riches of Christ.—Eph. iii. 8.

HOW shall I my Savior set forth?
   How shall I his beauties declare?
  Oh, how shall I speak of his worth,
   Or what his chief dignities are?

2 His angels can never express,
   Nor saints, who sit nearest his throne,
  How rich are his treasures of grace:
   Oh, no! 'tis a mystery unknown.

3 [In him all the fulness of God
   Forever transcendently shines;
  The Father's Anointed, he stood,
   To finish his glorious designs.]

4 Though once he was nailed to the cross;
   Vile rebels fast bound to set free,

His glory sustained no loss,—
    Eternal his kingdom shall be.

5 O sinners, believe and adore
    This Savior so rich to redeem!
  No creature can ever explore
    The treasures of goodness in him.

6 [Come, sinners, who see yourselves lost,
    And feel yourselves burdened with sin,
  Draw near while with terror you're tossed,
    Believe, and your peace shall begin.]

74   C. M. (Abridged.)   *Watts.*
The Divinity of Christ.

THEE we adore, Eternal Word!
    The Father's equal Son;
  By heaven's obedient hosts adored,
    Ere time its course begun.

2 The first creation has displayed
    Thine energy divine;
  For not a single thing was made
    By other hands than thine.

3 But ransomed sinners, with delight,
    Sublimer facts survey;
  The all-creating Word unites
    Himself to dust and clay.

4 See the Redeemer clothed in flesh,
    And ask the reason why:
  The answer fills my soul afresh,
    "To suffer, bleed, and die!"

5 God over all, forever blest,
    The righteous curse endures;
  And thus, to souls with sin distrest,
    Eternal bliss insures.

6 What wonders in thy person meet,
    My Savior, all divine!
  I fall with rapture at thy feet,
    And would be wholly thine.

75   7s.
Immanuel.—Matt. i. 23; 1 Tim. iii. 16.

GOD with us! Oh, glorious name!
  Let it shine in endless fame;
God and man in Christ unite;
Oh, mysterious depth and height!

2 God with us! amazing love
  Brought him from his courts above;
  Now, ye saints, his grace admire,
  Swell the song with holy fire.

3 God with us! but tainted not
  With the first transgressor's blot;
  Yet did he our sins sustain,
  Bear the guilt, the curse, the pain.

4 God with us! Oh, blissful theme!
   Let the impious not blaspheme;
   Jesus shall in judgment sit,
   Dooming rebels to the pit.

5 God with us! Oh, wondrous grace!
   Let us see him face to face,
   That we may Immanuel sing,
   As we ought, our God and King.

76　　　　　7s.　　　　*Vanmeter.*
Birth, Titles, and Kingdom of Christ.

"UNTO us a child is born;
　　Unto us a Son is given;
Praise him, all ye saints forlorn,
　　Praise him, all ye choirs of heaven!

2 On his shoulder shall be laid,
　　Rule, authority and power;
Kings and lords are subject made—
　　Nations shall the child adore!

3 Wonderful, his name shall be!
　　Counsellor, the mighty God!
Everlasting Father! he
　　Rules the nations with a rod.

4 He shall be the Prince of peace,
　　Reconciling men to God:
Full of truth, and full of grace;
　　He will cleanse us with his blood.

5 He shall sit on David's throne,
   And establish endless peace :
In his kingdom shall be known,
   Joys divine that never cease."

6 Jesus, Savior, we confess,
   And adore thy wondrous name!
May we realize thy grace,
   As thy praises we proclaim.

77   L. M.   *Watts.*
Glory and Grace in the Person of Christ.

NOW to the Lord a noble song!
   Awake, my soul, awake my tongue;
Hosanna to the eternal name,
And all his boundless love proclaim.

2 See where it shines in Jesus' face,
The brightest image of his grace;
God, in the person of his Son,
Has all his mightiest works outdone.

3 The spacious earth and spreading flood
Proclaim the wise, the powerful God;
And thy rich glories from afar
Sparkle in every rolling star.

4 But in his looks a glory stands,
The noblest labor of thy hands;
The pleasing lustre of his eyes
Outshines the wonders of the skies.

5 Grace, 'tis a sweet, a charming theme;
My thoughts rejoice at Jesus' name;
Ye angels, dwell upon the sound,
Ye heavens, reflect it to the ground!

6 Oh, may I live to reach the place
Where he unveils his lovely face,
Where all the beauties you behold,
And sing his name to harps of gold!

78 L. M. *Watts.*
Christ's Incarnation.

THE Lord is come, the heavens proclaim
His birth: the nations learn his name;
An unknown star directs the road
Of eastern sages to their God.

2 All ye bright armies of the skies,
Go worship where the Savior lies:
Angels and kings before him bow,
Those gods on high, and gods below.

3 Let idols totter to the ground,
And their own worshippers confound;
But Judah shout, but Zion sing,
And earth confess her sovereign King.

79 L. M. *Watts.*
Types and Prophecies of Christ.

BEHOLD the woman's promised seed!
Behold the great Messiah's come!

Behold the prophets all agreed
  To give him the superior room!

2 Abram, the saint, rejoiced of old,
    When visions of the Lord he saw;
  Moses, the man of God, foretold
    This great fulfiller of his law.

3 The types bore witness to his name,
    Obtained their chief design, and ceased;
  The incense and the bleeding lamb,
    The ark, the altar, and the priest.

4 Predictions in abundance meet
    To join their blessings on his head;
  Jesus, we worship at thy feet,
    And nations own the promised seed.

80   C. M.   *Watts.*

The Messiah's Coming and Kingdom.

JOY to the world; the Lord is come;
  Let earth receive her King;
Let every heart prepare him room,
  And heaven and nature sing.

2 Joy to the earth, the Savior reigns;
    Let men their songs employ;
  While fields and floods, rocks, hills, and plains,
    Repeat the sounding joy.

3 No more let sins and sorrows grow,
    Nor thorns infest the ground;

He comes to make his blessings flow
  Far as the curse is found.

4 He rules the world with truth and grace,
  And makes the nations prove
The glories of his righteousness,
  And wonders of his love.

81   S. M.   *Watts*
Christ's Mission.—John iii. 16, 17.

RAISE your triumphant songs
  To an immortal tune,
Let the wide earth resound the deeds
  Celestial grace has done.

2 Sing how eternal love
  Its chief beloved chose,
And bid him raise our wretched race
  From their abyss of woes.

3 His hand no thunder bears,
  No terror clothes his brow,
No bolts to drive our guilty souls
  To fiercer flames below.

4 'Twas mercy filled the throne,
  And wrath stood silent by,
When Christ was sent with mercy down
  To rebels doomed to die.

CHRIST—HIS INCARNATION AND BIRTH.

82   P. M.   *Heber.*
The Advent.

HAIL the blest morn! when the great Mediator
 Down from the mansions of glory descends,
Shepherds go worship the babe in the manger,
 Lo! for his guard the bright angels attend.

CHORUS.

Brightest and best of the sons of the morning
 Dawn on our darkness, and lend us thine aid;
Star in the east, the horizon adorning,
 Guide where our infant Redeemer is laid.

2 Cold on his cradle the dew-drops are shining,
 Low lies his head with the beasts of the stall;
Angels adore him, in slumbers reclining,
 Wise men and shepherds before him do fall.
  Brightest and best, &c.

3 Say, shall we yield him, in costly devotion,
 Odors of Eden, and offerings divine,
Gems from the mountains, and pearls from the ocean,
 Myrrh from the forest, and gold from the mine.
  Brightest and best, &c.

4 Vainly we offer each ample oblation,
    Vainly with gifts would his favor secure;
  Richer by far is the heart's adoration,
    Dearer to God are the prayers of the poor.
      Brightest and best, &c.

83   C. M.   *Dobell's Selec.*
  Nativity of Christ.—Luke ii. 8, 15.

WHILE shepherds watched their flocks by night,
    All seated on the ground,
  The angel of the Lord came down,
    And glory shone around.

2 "Fear not," said he, (for mighty dread
    Had seized their troubled mind;)
  "Glad tidings of great joy I bring
    To you and all mankind.

3 "To you, in David's town, this day
    Is born, of David's line,
  The SAVIOR, who is CHRIST the LORD:
    And this shall be the sign:

4 "The heavenly babe you there shall find,
    To human view displayed,
  All meanly wrapped in swathing-bands,
    And in a manger laid."

5 Thus spake the seraph; and forthwith
    Appeared a shining throng

Of angels praising God, who thus
  Addressed their joyful song:

6 "All glory be to God on high,
  And to the earth be peace;
Good-will, henceforth, from heaven to men
  Begin, and never cease."

84   L. M.   *Vanmeter.*
The Birth and Life of Christ.

COME, see the Lord's anointed King.
  Behold! he in a manger lies!
Raise your triumphant songs and sing:
  Extol his name above the skies!

2 See the young Prince at twelve years old,
  Amidst the doctors and the wise;
Such wisdom there he does unfold,
  As strikes the council with surprise.

3 Behold him go to Jordan's flood,
  To be immersed beneath its wave;
To teach obedience unto God,
  And represent his future grave.

4 But hark! he now proclaims abroad,
  The glorious news of gospel grace;
Commands the storm, controls the flood,
  And devils flee before his face!

5 At his command the dead arise,
  The blind, and lame, and halt are healed;

The law of God he magnifies,
  And thus his wondrous love revealed.

6 But be astonished, O my soul!
  The Savior dies that I might live!
He rose, and now exalted high,
  He has eternal life to give.

CHRIST—HIS LIFE AND CHARACTERS.

85   C. M.   *Watts.*

Angels Attending Christ and his Saints.

SOON as the Son of God had made
  His entrance on this earth,
A shining army downward fled,
  To celebrate his birth.

2 And when, oppressed with pains and fears,
  On the cold ground he lies,
Behold, a heavenly form appears
  To allay his agonies.

3 Now to the hands of Christ, our King,
  Are all their legions given;
They wait upon his saints, and bring
  His chosen heirs to heaven.

4 Pleasure and praise run through their host
    To see a sinner turn;
Then Satan has a captive lost,
    And Christ a subject born.

5 But there's an hour of brighter joy,
    When he his angels sends
Rebellious sinners to destroy,
    And gather in his friends.

5 Oh, could I say, without a doubt,
    "There shall my soul be found,"
Then let the great archangel shout,
    And the last trumpet sound.

86   C. M. (Abridged.)   *Stennett.*
Excellencies of Christ, &c.—Cant. v. 10, 16.

TO Christ the Lord let every tongue
    Its noblest tribute bring;
When he's the subject of the song,
    Who can refuse to sing?

2 Survey the beauties of his face,
    And on his glories dwell;
Think of the wonders of his grace,
    And all his triumphs tell.

3 Majestic sweetness sits enthroned
    Upon his awful brow;
His head with radiant glories crowned,
    His lips with grace o'erflow.

4 No mortal can with him compare
   Among the sons of men;
Fairer he is than all the fair
   That fill the heavenly train.

5 He saw me plunged in deep distress,
   He flew to my relief;
For me he bore the shameful cross,
   And carried all my grief.

6 Since from his bounty I receive
   Such proofs of love divine,
Had I a thousand hearts to give
   Lord, they should all be thine!

87   L. M.   Doddridge.
Christ's Transfiguration.—Matt. xvii.

WHEN at a distance, Lord, we trace
   The various glories of thy face,
What transport pours o'er all our breast,
And charms our cares and woes to rest?

2 With thee in the obscurest cell,
On some bleak mountain, would I dwell,
Rather than pompous courts behold,
And share their grandeur and their gold.

3 Away, ye dreams of mortal joy;
Raptures divine my thoughts employ;
I see the King of glory shine,
And feel his love, and call him mine.

s, will we sing his matchless name,
ith sweet delight, nor fear the shame;
him we'll boast, and sing, and talk,
ough fools deride and sinners mock.

C. M. *Watts.*

God reconciled in Christ.

DEAREST of all the names above,
My Jesus, and my God,
Who can resist thy heavenly love,
Or trifle with thy blood?

'Tis by the merits of thy death
The Father smiles again;
'Tis by thy interceding breath
The Spirit dwells with men.

Till God in human flesh I see,
My thoughts no comfort find;
The holy, just, and sacred Three
Are terrors to my mind.

But if Immanuel's face appear,
My hope, my joy begins;
His name forbids my slavish fear,
His grace removes my sins.

While Jews on their own laws rely,
And Greeks of wisdom boast,
I love the incarnate mystery,
And there I fix my trust.

90 C. M.

All in All.—Luke 2.

COMPARED with Christ, in all besides
  No comeliness I see;
The one thing needful, dearest Lord,
  Is to be one with thee.

2 The sense of thy expiring love
  Into my soul convey;
Thyself bestow; for thee alone,
  My *All in all*, I pray.

3 Less than thyself will not suffice
  My comfort to restore;
More than thyself I cannot crave,
  And thou canst give no more.

4 Loved of my God, for him again
  With love intense I'd burn;
Chosen of thee ere time began,
  I'd choose thee in return.

5 Whate'er consists not with thy love,
  Oh, teach me to resign;
I'm rich, to all the intents of bliss,
  If thou, O God, art mine.

91 L. M.

The Glory and Majesty of Christ.

THE glories of my Lord were told,
By holy men in days of old;

And ages yet to come, shall sing
The praise of this triumphant King.

Enthroned in heavenly majesty,
His face, with wonder, angels see;
The sun, and moon, and stars, with him,
Compared, appear but faint and dim.

Angels and seraphs tune the lyre,
And men redeemed his love admire;
In heaven and earth his name is sung,
The burden of creation's tongue.

While sinners feed upon the wind,
And feast their vain and carnal mind;
My soul would gaze on Jesus' face,
And taste the riches of his grace.

L. M. Steele.

All in All.—Col. iii. 11.

In Christ I've all my soul desires;
His Spirit does my heart inspire
With boundless wishes large and high,
And Christ will all my wants supply.

Christ is my rock, my steady hand guide;
For in his blood my soul is justified;
He is my way to heaven on high,
He is my soul's supreme felicity.

Christ is the sum of all my bliss,
My wisdom and my righteousness;

My Savior, Brother, and my Friend,
On him alone I now depend.

4 Christ is my King, to rule and bless,
And all my troubles to redress;
He's my salvation and my all,
Whate'er on earth shall me befall.

5 Christ is my strength and portion too;
My soul in him can all things do;
Through him I'll triumph o'er the grave,
And death and hell my soul outbrave.

93   S. M.   Hos.

Bread of Life.—John vi. 35, 48, 51.

BEHOLD the gift of God!
  Come, saints, adore his name!
Who shed for us his precious blood,
  Who bore our curse and shame.

2 Behold the living bread!
  Which Jesus came to give,
By dying in the sinner's stead,
  That he might ever live.

3 Behold the Savior's love!
  Who gives his flesh to eat;
Never did people taste above
  Provisions half so sweet.

4 The Lord delights to give:
  He knows you've naught to buy;

2 Jesus, thou art the living bread
By which our needy souls are fed;
In thee alone thy children find
Enough to fill the empty mind.

3 Without this bread I starve and die;
No other can my need supply;
But this will suit my wretched case,
Abroad, at home, in every place.

4 'Tis this relieves the hungry poor,
Who ask for bread at mercy's door;
This living food descends from heaven,
As manna to the Jews was given.

5 This precious food my heart revives;
What strength, what nourishment, it gives!
Oh, let me evermore be fed
With this divine, celestial bread.

96   L. M.   *Fawcett.*
Bridegroom.

JESUS, the heavenly Lover, gave
His life a wretched soul to save;
Ready to make his mercy known,
He kindly claims me for his own.

2 Rebellious I against him strove,
Till moved and constrained by love;
With sin and self I freely part,
The heavenly bridegroom wins my heart.

3 My guilt, my wretchedness, he knows.
  Yet takes and owns me for his spouse:
  My debts he pays, and sets me free.
  And makes his riches o'er to me.

4 My filthy rags are laid aside,
  He clothes me as becomes his bride;
  Himself bestows my wedding dress,—
  The robe of perfect righteousness.

5 Lost in astonishment, I see,
  Jesus! thy boundless love to me:
  With angels I thy grace adore.
  And long to love and praise thee more.

6 Since thou wilt take me for thy bride,
  O Savior, keep me near thy side!
  I fain would give thee all my heart,
  Nor ever from my Lord depart.

97   L. M.   *Vanmeter.*

Jesus, our only Hope.

LORD, unto whom should sinners go?
  Thou hast the words of endless life:
When sinking down with grief and wo.
  Thy voice affords us quick relief.

2 Thou hast all power in heaven above.
  And all below the shining sun;
  The earth. and all the worlds that move.
  Are subject to thy lofty throne.

3 When we beheld our lost estate,
    We sought for pardon in thy name;
And as a tower of retreat,
    We ran to thee, our bleeding lamb.

4 Amidst temptations, sharp and long,
    And tribulations here below;
Thy name is like a fortress strong
    To which thy tempted children go.

5 When clouds and darkness veil the way,
    And doubts and fears our souls annoy,
Thy presence turns our night to day,
    And all our doubts and fears to joy.

6 O, may the savor of thy name
    Afford us sweet relief in death;
Give us the victory o'er the same
    When we resign our fleeting breath!

98   S. 7.   *Madan's Col.*

Consolation of Israel.—Luke ii. 25.

COME, thou long expected Jesus!
    Born to set thy people free;
From our fears and sins release us,
    Let us find our rest in thee:
Israel's strength and consolation,
    Hope of all the saints thou art;
Dear desire of every nation,
    Joy of every longing heart.

2 Born thy people to deliver:
   Born a child and yet a king;
   Born to reign in us forever,
   Now thy gracious kingdom bring.
   By thy own eternal Spirit,
   Rule in all our hearts alone;
   By thy all-sufficient merit,
   Raise us to thy glorious throne.

99   C. M.   *Doddridge*
   The Door.—John x. 9; Hosea ii. 15.

AWAKE, our souls, and bless his name
   Whose mercies never fail;
Who opens wide a door of hope
   In Achor's gloomy vale.

2 Behold the portal wide displayed,
   The building strong and fair;
  With leaves pastured fresh and green,
   And living fountains are there.

3 Enter, my soul, with cheerful haste,
   [...]
   [...]
   [...]

4 Oh [...] the nations look,
   And Jews and Gentiles come,
   All [...] through one beauteous gate
   To our eternal home.

CHRIST.

11s.   *Vanmeter.*

"The name of the Lord is a Strong Tower."

THE name of the Lord is my tower of defence;
  My Rock, my foundation, my strong con-
      fidence;
My sword and my helmet, in whom I will boast,
My shield and my buckler, my joy and my trust.

He is my great shepherd, and I shall be fed;
His blood is my drink, and his flesh is my bread;
My saviour and my husband, my priest and my
      king,
My prophet to teach and my theme for to sing.

Yea, he is my wisdom and my righteousness,
My sanctification and my hiding place;
He is my redemption, my way and my end,
My mediator, my captain, my judge and my friend.

He is the great refuge to which I repair,
When trials and troubles, and dangers appear;
And when I'm in darkness he is the great sun
That scatters my clouds and turns night into

101 C. M.

Door.—John x. 9.

CHRIST is the way to heaven alight,
 And Christ the only door;
My soul, pursue no way but this,
 For this alone is sure.

2 'Tis through this door, and through alone,
 That thou art led to God:
Then rest on what thy Lord has done,
 And plead his precious blood.

3 [Jesus will guide thee on to heaven
 And give thee entrance in;
And God will own thy sins forgiven,
 However vile they've been.

102 C. M.

Jesus, our only Theme.

JESUS! O, what a wondrous theme
 For mortal tongues to sound;
Awake my heart to sing his name,
 And make his praise resound.

2 Jesus! a Savior, born to die,
 That I, a wretch, might live;
He rose, and now above the sky
 Hath endless life to give!

3 He saw me bound in chains of sin,
 And on the downward road;

CHRIST.

And gave his life to ransom mine,
  And bring me home to God.

Jesus! the name I love so well,
  Let all the ......
And saint above ....
  And endless praise ....!

93   C. M.   Watts.
Christ the Foundation.

BEHOLD the sure foundation-stone,
  Which God in Zion lays
To build our heavenly hopes upon,
  And his eternal praise.

2 Chosen of God, to sinners ....,
  And saints adore the name;
They trust their whole salvation here,
  Nor shall they suffer shame.

3 The foolish builders, scribe and priest,
  Reject it with disdain;
Yet on this rock the church shall rest,
  And envy rage in vain.

4 What though the gates of hell withstood,
  Yet must this building rise;
'Tis thy own work, Almighty God,
  And wondrous in our eyes.

104   C. M   *Cowper.*

The Fountain Opened.—Zech. xiii. 1.

THERE is a fountain filled with blood,
    Drawn from Immanuel's veins,
And sinners plunged beneath that flood,
    Lose all their guilty stains.

2 The dying thief rejoiced to see
    That fountain in his day;
And there may I, though vile as he,
    Wash all my sins away.

3 Dear dying Lamb, thy precious blood
    Shall never lose its power
Till all the ransomed church of God
    Be saved, to sin no more.

4 E'er since by faith I saw the stream
    Thy flowing wounds supply,
Redeeming love has been my theme,
    And shall be till I die.

5 Then, in a nobler, sweeter song,
    I'll sing thy power to save,
When this poor, lisping, stammering tongue
    Lies silent in the grave.

6 Lord, I believe thou hast prepared
    (Unworthy though I be)
For me a blood-bought, free reward,
    A golden harp for me.

7 'Tis strung and tuned for endless years,
    And formed by power divine,
To sound in God the Father's ears
    No other name but thine:

8 In heavenly strains, from every chord,
    Still flow the charming sound,
The praise of my redeeming Lord,
    While angels wonder round.

165   L. M.   *Newton.*

Friend.

1 POOR, weak, and worthless though I am,
    I have a rich, almighty friend,
Jesus, the Savior, is his name,
    He freely loves, and without end.

2 He ransomed me from hell with blood,
    And, by his power, my foes controlled;
He found me wandering far from God,
    And brought me to his chosen fold.

3 He cheers my heart, my wants supplies,
    And says that I shall shortly be
Enthroned with him above the skies:
    Oh, what a friend is Christ to me!

166   L. M.   *Beddome.*

Gift of God.—John iii. 16; 2 Cor. ix. 15.

1 JESUS, my love, my chief delight,
    For thee I long, for thee I pray,

Amid the shadows of the night,
   Amid the business of the day!

2 When shall I see thy smiling face,—
   That face which I have often seen?
 Arise thou Sun of Righteousness,
   Scatter the clouds that intervene!

3 Thou art the glorious gift of God
   To sinners weary and distrest;
 The first of all his gifts bestowed,
   And certain pledge of all the rest.

4 Could I but say this gift is mine,
   I'd tread the world beneath my feet,
 No more at poverty repine,
   Nor envy the rich sinner's state.

5 The precious jewel I would keep,
   And lodge it deep within my heart;
 At home, abroad, awake, asleep,
   It never should from thence depart.

107   L. M.   *Vanmeter.*
Jesus, the one Thing Needful.

"ONE thing is needful," saith the Lord!
   "One pearl," a pearl of price unknown:
 Nor earth, nor heaven can afford,
   A source of joy but this alone.

2 Jesus, this one thing needful is;
   Behold, in him what riches dwell!

An ocean of undying bliss
  Is found in our Immanuel!

3 Well might an humble Mary choose
    Such honor and such company!
  While Greeks and unbelieving Jews,
    Could in her Lord no beauties see.

4 He loved her first, and won her heart,
    By his amazing, sovereign love;
  And now she cannot from him part,
    But longs to reign with him above.

5 Lord, may I choose, like her, to sit
    And hear thy wondrous words of grace;
  I'd humbly lie at Jesus' feet,
    Could I but gaze upon his face!

108   C. M.   *Doddridge.*
Head of the Church.—Eph. iv. 15, 16.

JESUS, I sing thy matchless grace
  That calls a worm thy own,
Gives me among thy saints a place
  To make thy glories known.

2 Allied to thee, our vital head,
    We act, and grow, and thrive;
  From thee divided, each is dead
    When most he seems alive.

3 Thy saints on earth, and those above,
    Here join in sweet accord;

One body all in mutual love,
  And thou our common Lord.

4 Oh, may my faith each hour derive
  Thy spirit with delight;
While death and hell in vain shall strive
  This bond to disunite.

5 Thou the whole body will present
  Before thy Father's face,
Nor shall a wrinkle or a spot
  Its beauteous form disgrace.

109   L. M.   *Doddridge.*
Corner-Stone.—1 Pet. ii. 6; Isa. xxviii. 16.

LORD, dost thou show a corner-stone
  For us to build our hopes upon,
That the fair edifice may rise
Sublime in light beyond the skies?

2 We own the work of sovereign love;
Nor death nor hell the hopes shall move
Which fixed on this foundation stand,
Laid by thy own almighty hand.

3 Thy people long this stone have tried,
And all the powers of hell defied;
Floods of temptation beat in vain,
Well doth this rock the house sustain.

4 When storms of wrath around prevail,
Whirlwind and thunder, fire and hail,
'Tis here our trembling souls shall hide,
And here securely they abide:

5 While such as scorn this precious stone,
Fond of some quicksand of their own,
Borne down by weighty vengeance die,
And buried deep in ruin lie.

110   L. M.   *Medley.*

The Believer's Hiding-Place.

HAIL, sovereign love, that first began
The scheme to rescue fallen man!
Hail, matchless, free, eternal grace,
That gave my soul a hiding-place.

2 Against the God that rules the sky
I fought with hands uplifted high,
Despised the gospel of his grace,
Too proud to seek a hiding-place.

3 Enwrapped in dark Egyptian night,
Fonder of darkness than of light,
Madly I ran the sinful race,
Secure without a hiding-place.

4 But thus the eternal counsel ran:
"Almighty Love, arrest the man!"
I felt the arrows of distress,
And found I had no hiding-place.

5 Vindictive justice stood in view;
  To Sinai's fiery mount I flew,
  But justice cried, with frowning face,
  "This mountain is no hiding-place."

6 But lo! a heavenly voice I heard,
  And mercy for my soul appeared,
  Which lead me on a pleasing pace
  To Jesus as my hiding-place.

111.   11s.   *Christian Psalmist.*
        Jacob's Ladder.

WHEN Jacob, the pilgrim, was wearied by day,
At night on a stone for a pillow he lay,
And saw in a vision a ladder so high,
Its foot was on earth, and its top in the sky.

CHORUS.

Hallelujah to Jesus who died on the tree,
To raise up this ladder of mercy for me,
Press upward, press upward, the prize is in view;
A crown of bright glory is waiting for you.

2 This heavenly ladder is strong and well made,
  Has lasted for ages, and is not decayed;
  The feeblest may venture with faith to go up,
  And angels will help them from bottom to top.
    Hallelujah, &c.

3 Lo! upward and downward they constantly go,
  Extending a hand to the toilers below;
  And when a new climber sets out for the skies,
  Then shouts to the top of the ladder arise.
    Hallelujah, &c.

4 "Another, another," they sing, in their love,
  "Is seeking his home and his treasure above,"
  And angels in glory, responding, cry "Come,"
  And welcome each penitent sinner up home.
    Hallelujah, &c.

5 This ladder is Jesus, the glorious God-man,
  Whose blood freely streaming from Calvary ran;
  By *his* great atonement to heaven we rise,
  And sing in the mansions prepared in the skies.
    Hallelujah, &c.

6 Come, sin-burdened brother, ascend with your load;
  No—leave it behind you, and rise up to God;
  Set foot on the ladder, and soon you will find,
  The troublesome burden of sin left behind.
    Hallelujah, &c.

112　　　　　L. M.　　　　*Newton.*

Jesus—"The Virgins love thee."—Cant. i. 3.

HOW sweet the name of Jesus sounds
  In a believer's ear!
It soothes his sorrows, heals his wounds,
  And drives away his fear.

2 It makes the wounded spirit whole,
   And calms the troubled breast;
  'Tis manna to the hungry soul,
   And to the weary rest.

3 Dear name! the rock on which I build,
   My shield and hiding-place,
  My never-failing treasury, filled
   With stores of boundless grace.

4 Jesus, my Shepherd, Husband, Friend,
   My Prophet, Priest, and King,
  My Lord, my Life, my Way, my End,
   Accept the praise I bring.

5 Weak is the effort of my heart,
   And cold my warmest thought;
  But when I see thee as thou art
   I'll praise thee as I ought.

6 Till then I would thy love proclaim
   With every fleeting breath,
  And may the music of thy name
   Refresh my soul in death.

113   L. M.   *Watt's Lyrics.*
Love to Christ, present or absent.

OF all the joys we mortals know,
   Jesus, thy love exceeds the rest;
 Love, the best blessing here below,
   The nearest image of the blest.

CHRIST.

2 While we are held in thy embrace,
  There's not a thought attempts to rove;
Each smile upon thy beauteous face
  Fixes, and charms, and fires our love.

3 While of thy absence we complain,
  And long or weep in all we do,
There's a strange pleasure in the pain,
  And tears have their own sweetness too.

4 When round thy courts by day we rove,
  Or ask the watchmen of the night
For some kind tidings of our love,
  Thy very name creates delight.

5 Jesus, our God, yet rather come!
  Our eyes would dwell upon thy face;
'Tis best to see our Lord at home
  And feel the presence of his grace.

114 L. M. *Steele.*

Shepherd.

WHILE my Redeemer's near,
  My Shepherd and my Guide,
I bid farewell to anxious fear,
  My wants are all supplied.

2 To ever-fragrant meads,
  Where rich abundance grows,
His gracious hand indulgent leads,
  And guards my sweet repose.

3 Along the lovely scene
    Cool waters gently roll,
  Transparent, sweet, and all serene,
    To cheer my fainting soul.

4 Here let my spirit rest;
    How sweet a lot is mine!
  With pleasure, food, and safety blest;
    Beneficence divine!

5 Dear Shepherd, if I stray,
    My wandering feet restore;
  To thy fair pastures guide my way,
    And let me rove no more.

6 Unworthy as I am
    Of thy protecting care,
  Jesus, I plead thy gracious name,
    For all my hopes are there.

115   7s.   *Hill's Col.*

Seeking the Shepherd's Little Flock.—Cant. i. 7.

TELL me, Savior, from above,
  Dearest object of my love,
Where thy little flock abide,
Sheltered near thy bleeding side?

2 Tell me, Shepherd all divine,
  Where I may my soul recline;
  Where for refuge shall I fly,
  While the burning sun is high?

3 [Wilt thou let me run astray,
  Mourning, grieving all the day?
  Wilt thou bear to see me rove,
  Seeking base and mortal love?

4 Never had I sought thy name,
  Never felt the inward flame,
  Had not love first touched my heart,
  Given the painful, pleasing smart.]

5 Didst thou leave thy glorious throne,
  Put a mortal raiment on,
  As a cursed victim die,
  For a wretch so vile as I?

6 Turn and claim me as thine own;
  Be my portion, Lord, alone;
  Deign to hear a sinner's call,
  Be my everlasting All.

116 L. M. *Cennick.*
Way to Canaan.—Isa. xxxv. 8, 10.

JESUS, my all, to heaven is gone,
  He whom I fix my hopes upon;
His track I see, and I'll pursue
The narrow way till him I view.

2 The way the holy prophets went,
  The road that leads from banishment,—
  The king's highway of holiness,—
  I'll go; for all his paths are peace.

3 This is the way I long have sought,
 And mourned because I found it not;
 My grief, my burden long has been,
 Because I could not cease from sin.

4 The more I strove against its power,
 I sinned and stumbled but the more:
 Till late I heard my Savior say,
 "Come hither, soul, I am the way,"

5 Lo, glad I come, and thou, blest Lamb,
 Shalt take me to thee as I am!
 My sinful self to thee I give:
 Nothing but love shall I receive.

6 Then will I tell to sinners round
 What a dear Savior I have found;
 I'll point to thy redeeming blood,
 And say, "Behold the way to God!"

117　　　　　S. M.　　　　　*Watts.*

Christ, the Wisdom of God.—Prov. viii. 1, 22, 32.

SHALL Wisdom cry aloud,
 　And not her speech be heard?
 The voice of God's eternal word,
 　Deserves it no regard?

2 "I was his chief delight,
 　His everlasting Son,
 Before the first of all his works,
 　Creation was begun.

3 ["Before the flying clouds,
  Before the solid land,
Before the fields, before the floods,
  I dwelt at his right hand.

4 "When he adorned the skies,
  And built them, I was there
To order when the sun should rise,
  And marshal every star.

5 "When he poured out the sea,
  And spread the flowing deep,
I gave the flood a firm decree
  In its own bounds to keep.]

6 "Upon the empty air
  The earth was balanced well;
With joy I saw the mansion where
  The sons of men should dwell.

7 "My busy thoughts at first
  On their salvation ran,
Ere sin was born, or Adam's dust
  Was fashioned to a man.

8 "Then come, receive my grace,
  Ye children, and be wise;
Happy the man that keeps my ways;
  The man that shuns them dies."

118   7s.   *Toplady.*
Rock of Ages.—Isaiah xxvi. 4.

ROCK of ages! shelter me!
  Let me hide myself in thee!

Let the water and the blood,
From thy wounded side which flowed,
Be of sin the double cure;
Cleanse me from its guilt and power.

2 Not the labor of my hands
Can fulfill thy law's demands;
Could my zeal no respite know,
Could my tears forever flow;
All for sin could not atone:
Thou must save, and thou alone.

3 Nothing in my hand I bring,
Simply to thy cross I cling;
Naked, come to thee for dress,
Helpless, look to thee for grace;
Black, I to thy fountain fly,
Wash me, Savior, or I die.

4 While I draw this fleeting breath,
When my eye-strings break in death;
When I soar to worlds unknown,
See thee on thy Judgment throne;
Rock of Ages, shelter me!
Let me hide myself in thee!

119   11s.   *Bennett.*
Lead me to the Rock.—Ps. lxi. 2.

CONVINCED as a sinner, to Jesus I come,
Informed by the gospel for such there is room;
Overwhelmed with sorrow for sin, will I cry,
"Lead me to the Rock that is higher than I."

2 When tempted by Satan my Savior to leave,
   Who sets forth religion as meant to deceive,
   I'll claim my relation to Jesus on high,
   The Rock of Salvation that's higher than I!

3 When God from my soul shall his presence remove,
   To try by his absence the strength of my love,
   I'll rest on the promise of Jesus, and try
   The force of that rock which is higher than I!

4 When sorely afflicted and ready to faint,
   Before my Redeemer I'll spread my complaint;
   Midst storms and distresses, my soul shall rely
   On Jesus, the Rock that is higher than I!

5 When summoned by death before God to appear,
   Thy free grace supporting, I'll yield without fear;
   Most gladly I'll venture with Jesus on high
   To enter the Rock that is higher than I!

6 'Tis there, with the chosen of Jesus, I long
   To dwell, and eternally join in the song
   Of praising and blessing, with angels on high,
   Christ Jesus, the Rock that is higher than I!

120   L. M.   *Vanmeter.*
Jesus, the Theme of Praise.

O HOW delightful is the theme,
   How sweet the sound of Jesus' name!

His wisdom and his boundless grace
Exceed our highest songs of praise.

2 He saw his people captive led,
In sin and in trespasses dead;
He broke the chains by Satan bound,
And gave his head a dreadful wound.

3 He died to set us prisoners free,
And rose with palms of victory;
And when he rose he conquered hell,
And all the powers of darkness fell.

4 For them he lived, for them he died;
With him their sins were crucified;
For them he rose and did ascend,
Their intercessor and their friend.

5 Dear Savior, for such boundless grace,
Receive the tribute of our praise:
We would, but we can do no more,
Than love, and wonder, and adore!

CHRIST'S SUFFERINGS AND DEATH.

121   L. M.   *Watts.*
Christ's Passion and Sinners' Salvation.

DEEP in our hearts let us record
The deeper sorrows of our Lord;
Behold the rising billows roll
To overwhelm his holy soul.

2 In long complaints he spends his breath,
While hosts of hell, and powers of death,
And all the sons of malice, join
To execute their cursed design.

3 Yet, gracious God, thy power and love
Have made the curse a blessing prove;
Those dreadful sufferings of thy Son
Atoned for sins which we had done.

4 The pangs of our expiring Lord
The honors of thy law restored;
His sorrows made thy justice known,
And paid for follies not his own.

5 Oh, for his sake our guilt forgive
And let the mourning sinner live;

The Lord will hear us in his name,
Nor shall our hope be turned to shame.

122 L. M. *Primitive.*
Gethsemane.

'TIS midnight!—and on Olive's brow
　The star is dimmed that lofty shone;
'Tis midnight!—in the garden now
　The suffering Savior prays alone.

2 'Tis midnight!—and from all removed,
　Immanuel wrestles lone with fears;
E'en the disciple that he loved
　Heeds not his Master's grief and tears.

3 'Tis midnight!—and for others' guilt
　The Man of Sorrows weeps in blood;
Yet he that hath in anguish knelt,
　Is not forsaken by his God.

4 'Tis midnight!—from the heavenly plains
　Is borne the songs that angels know;
Unheard by mortals are the strains
　That sweetly soothe the Savior's woe.

123 L. M. *Stennett.*
Attraction of the Cross.

YONDER—amazing sight!—I see
　The incarnate Son of God
Expiring on the fatal tree
　And weltering in his blood.

2 Behold a purple torrent run
   Down from his hands and head:
The crimson tide puts out the sun;
   His groans awake the dead.

3 The trembling earth, the darkened sky,
   Proclaim the truth aloud;
And with the amazed centurion cry,
   "This is the Son of God."

4 So great, so vast a sacrifice
   May well my hope revive:
If God's own Son thus bleeds and dies,
   The sinner sure may live.

5 Oh that these cords of love divine
   Might draw me, Lord, to thee!
Thou hast my heart, it shall be thine,—
   Thine it shall ever be.

124 L. M. *Vanmeter.*
Christ on the Cross.

LOOK down, with wonder and surprise,
   Ye waiting angels round the throne!
Lo! who is this that bleeds and dies?
   'Tis God's beloved, darling Son!

2 Lo! what a sight! the Lamb divine,
   In death bows his majestic head!
Well may the sun refuse to shine,
   And blush to see the Savior bleed!

3 Well may the earth's foundations shake;
　　Well may the graves give up their dead;
　Well may the rocks asunder break,
　　While vengeance pours upon his head!

4 Oh! dreadful, yet auspicious day!
　　Oh! costly price, yet glorious end!
　He dies the sinner's debt to pay!
　　Oh! Who is like the sinner's friend!

5 But now, the glorious work is done,
　　God's righteous law is satisfied;
　He rises and ascends his throne,
　　An intercessor for his bride.

6 Exalted now at God's right hand,
　　He pleads the merit of his blood;
　Till all his saints from every land,
　　Shall be conducted home to God.

125　　　　　L. M.　　　　　*Watts.*
Christ Dying, Rising, and Reigning.—Rom. iv. 25.

HE dies! the Friend of sinners dies!
　　Lo! Salem's daughters weep around!
　A solemn darkness veils the skies!
　　A sudden trembling shakes the ground!

2 Come saints, and drop a tear or two
　　For him who groaned beneath your load;
　He shed a thousand drops for you,
　　A thousand drops of richer blood!

3 Here's love and grief beyond degree!
    The Lord of glory dies for men!
But lo! What sudden joys we see!
    Jesus from death revives again!

4 The rising God forsakes the tomb!
    Up to his Father's court he flies;
Cherubic legions guard him home,
    And shout him welcome to the skies!

5 Break off your tears, ye saints, and tell
    How high our great Deliverer reigns!
Sing how he spoiled the hosts of hell,
    And led the monster, death, in chains!

6 Say, "Live forever, wondrous King,
    Born to redeem, and strong to save!"
Then ask the monster, "Where's thy sting?
    And where's thy victory, boasting grave?"

126   L. M.   *Watts.*

*Crucifixion to the World by the Cross of Christ.—
Gal. vi. 14.*

WHEN I survey the wondrous cross
    On which the Prince of Glory died,
My richest gain I count but loss,
    And pour contempt on all my pride.

2 Forbid it, Lord, that I should boast,
    Save in the death of Christ my God;
All the vain things that charm me most,
    I sacrifice them to his blood.

3 See from his head, his hands, his feet,
   Sorrow and love flow mingled down:
Did e'er such love and sorrow meet?
   Or thorns compose so rich a crown?

4 [His dying crimson, like a robe,
   Spreads o'er his body on the tree,
Then am I dead to all the globe,
   And all the globe is dead to me.]

5 Were the whole realm of nature mine,
   That were a present far too small;
Love so amazing, so divine,
   Demands my soul, my life, my all.

127   C. M.   *Watts.*
Godly sorrow arising from the sufferings of Christ.

ALAS! and did my Savior bleed,
   And did my Sovereign die?
Would he devote that sacred head
   For such a worm as I?

2 [Thy body slain, sweet Jesus, thine,
   And bathed in its own blood,
While all exposed to wrath divine
   The glorious sufferer stood.]

3 Was it for crimes that I had done
   He groaned upon the tree?
Amazing pity! grace unknown!
   And love beyond degree!

4 Well might the sun in darkness hide,
   And shut his glories in,

When Christ, the Lord, our Saviour died
For man the creature's sin.

5 Thus might I hide my blushing face
While his dear cross appears,
Dissolve my heart in thankfulness,
And melt mine eyes in tears.

6 But drops of grief can ne'er repay
The debt of love I owe;
Here, Lord, I give myself away;
'Tis all that I can do.

128   C. M.   *Stennett.*
The Converted Thief.—Luke xxiii. 42.

AS on the cross the Savior hung,
And wept, and bled, and died,
He poured salvation on a wretch
That languished at his side.

2 His crimes, with inward grief and shame,
The penitent confessed;
Then turned his dying eyes to Christ,
And thus his prayer addressed:

3 "Jesus, thou Son and heir of heaven,
Thou spotless Lamb of God,
I see thee bathed in sweat and tears,
And weltering in thy blood.

4 Yet quickly from these scenes of woe
In triumph thou shalt rise,

Burst through the gloomy shades of death,
  And shine above the skies.

5 Amid the glories of that world,
  Dear Savior, think on me,
And in the victories of thy death
  Let me a sharer be."

6 His prayer the dying Jesus hears,
  And instantly replies,—
To-day thy parting soul shall be
  With me in Paradise.

129   C. M.   *Swain.*
        Canticles ii. 1.

THE finest flower that ever blowed,
  Opened on Calvary's tree,
When Jesus' blood in rivers flowed,
  For love of worthless me!

2 Its deepest hue, its richest smell,
  No mortal can declare;
Nor can the tongue of angels tell
  How bright the colors are.

3 Earth could not hold so rich a flower,
  Nor half its beauties show,
Nor could the world and Satan's power
  Confine its sweets below.

4 On Canaan's banks, supremely fair,
  This flower of glory blooms;
Transplanted to its native air,
  And all the shores perfumes.

5 But not to Canaan's shores confined;
　The seeds which from it blow,
Take root within the human mind,
　And scent the church below.

6 And soon on yonder banks above,
　Shall every blossom here
Appear a full blown flower of love,
　Like him, transplanted there.

120　　　　　L. M.　　　　　*Stennett*
It is Finished.—John xix. 30.

'TIS finished! so the Savior cried,
And meekly bowed his head and died;
'Tis finished!—yes, the race is run,
The battle fought, the victory won.

2 'Tis finished!—all that heaven decreed,
And all the ancient prophets said,
Is now fulfilled, as was designed,
In me, the Savior of mankind.

3 'Tis finished—Aaron now no more
Must stain his robes with purple gore;
The sacred vail is rent in twain,
And Jewish rites no more remain.

4 'Tis finished!—this, my dying groan,
Shall sin of every kind atone:
Millions shall be redeemed from death
By this, my last, expiring breath.

5 'Tis finished!—Heaven is reconciled,
And all the powers of darkness spoiled,
Peace, love, and happiness again
Return and dwell with sinful men.

6 'Tis finished!—let the joyful sound
Be heard through all the nations round:
'Tis finished!—let the echo fly
Through heaven and hell, through earth and sky.

131 S. M. *Watts.*
Christ's Humiliation and Reward.

LIKE sheep we went astray,
  And broke the fold of God,
Each wandering in a different way,
  But all the downward road.

2 How dreadful was the hour
  When God our wanderings laid,
And did at once his vengeance pour
  Upon the Shepherd's head!

3 How glorious was the grace
  When Christ sustained the stroke!
His life and blood the Shepherd pays
  A ransom for the flock.

4 His honor and his breath
  Were taken both away;
Joined with the wicked in his death,
  And made as vile as they.

CHRIST'S SUFFERINGS AND DEATH.

5 But God shall raise his head
   O'er all the sons of men,
And make him see a numerous seed
   To recompense his pain.

6 I'll give him (saith the Lord)
   A portion with the strong;
He shall possess a large reward,
   And hold his honors long.

132　　　　L. M.　　　*Presby. Selec.*
The Law Satisfied by Christ's Death.

WHEN on the cross my Savior died,
　God's holy law is satisfied;
My debts he paid, my sins he bore,
And justice now demands no more.

2 A healing balm his hand bestows,
To cure my wounds and ease my woes;
And a rich fountain still remains,
To wash away my guilty stains.

3 Here will I bathe my guilty soul,
Here blessings without number roll;
My hopes and joys I hence derive,
For Jesus died that I might live.

133　　　　L. M.　　　*Watts.*
The Priesthood of Christ.—Luke xxiii. 34.

BLOOD has a voice to pierce the skies;
　"Revenge!" the blood of Abel cries;

CHRIST'S SUFFERINGS AND DEATH. 123

But the dear stream, when Christ was slain,
Speaks peace as loud from every vein.

2 Pardon and peace from God on high;
Behold, he lays his vengeance by;
And rebels that deserve his sword,
Become the favorites of the Lord.

3 To Jesus let our praises rise,
Who gave his life a sacrifice;
Now he appears before our God,
And for our pardon pleads his blood.

134   C. M.
The Believer Near the Cross.

MY Savior! on Mount Calvary,
   And near thy cross I stand:
The most delightful place to me
   In all Judea's land.

2 In those pierced hands, and feet, and side,
   And that distressed face,
With reverence let me always view
   The Lord, my righteousness.

3 And were those pains endured for me?
   Lord, help my feeble tongue
To spread the wonders of thy love
   In a melodious song.

CHRIST'S SUFFERINGS AND DEATH.

135   C. M.   *Watts.*
My Sins have Crucified Him.

INFINITE grief! amazing wo!
   Behold my bleeding Lord!
Hell and the Jews conspire his death
   And use the Roman sword.

2 O the sharp pangs of smarting pain
   My dear Redeemer bore!
When knotty whips and jagged thorns
   His sacred body tore!

3 But knotty whips and jagged thorns
   In vain do I accuse:
In vain I blame the Roman bands,
   And the more spiteful Jews.

4 'Twere you, my sins, my cruel sins,
   His chief tormentors were;
Each of my crimes became a nail,
   And unbelief, a spear.

136   L. M.   *Perry.*
It is Christ that Died.—Rom. viii. 34.

SINNERS, rejoice, it's Christ that died;
Behold, the blood flows from his side,
To wash your souls and raise you high,
To dwell with God above the sky.

2 It's Christ that died, oh, love divine!
   Here mercy, truth, and justice shine;

God reconciled, and sinners bought
With Jesus' blood: how sweet the thought!

3 It's Christ that died, a truth indeed
On which my faith would ever feed:
Nor let the works that I perform
Be named, to swell a haughty worm.

4 It's Christ that died, it's Christ was slain,
To save my soul from endless pain;
It's Christ that died shall be my theme
While I have breath to praise his name.

CHRIST'S RESURRECTION AND ASCENSION.

137 7s. *Presby. Selec.*
Praise to the Risen Redeemer.

LO! the stone is rolled away,
Death yields up his mighty prey;
Jesus, rising from the tomb,
Scatters all its fearful gloom.

2 Praise him, ye celestial choirs,
Praise and sweep your golden lyres;
Praise him in the noblest songs
From ten thousand thousand tongues.

3 Every note with rapture swell,
   And the Savior's triumph tell;
   Where, O death, is now thy sting?
   Where thy terrors, vanquished king?

4 Let Immanuel be adored,
   Ransom, Mediator, Lord!
   To creation's utmost bound
   Let the eternal praise resound.

138*   C. M.   *Doddridge*

Comfort to those who seek a risen Jesus.—Matt xxviii. 5, 6.

YE humble souls that seek the Lord,
   Chase all your fears away,
And bow with pleasure down to see
   The place where Jesus lay.

2 Thus low the Lord of life was brought;
   Such wonders love can do!
Thus cold in death that bosom lay
   Which throbbed and bled for you.

3 Then dry your tears and tune your songs,
   The Savior lives again;
Not all the bolts and bars of death
   The Conqueror could detain.

4 High o'er the angelic bands he rears
   His once dishonored head,

And through unnumbered years he reigns
  Who dwelt among the dead.

5 With joy like his shall every saint
  His empty tomb survey,
Then rise, with his ascending Lord,
  To realms of endless day.

139   8s.   *Virginia Selec.*
Christ's Resurrection the Saints' Triumph.

THE angels that watched round the tomb
  Where low the Redeemer was laid,
When deep in mortality's gloom
  He hid for a season his head;
That veiled their fair face while he slept,
  And ceased their sweet harps to employ,
Have witnessed his rising and swept
  The chords with the triumph of joy.

Ye saints, who once languished below,
  But long since have entered your rest,
I pant to be glorified too,
  To lean on Immanuel's breast!
The grave in which Jesus was laid
  Has buried my guilt and my fears;
And while I contemplate its shade,
  The light of his presence appears.

Oh, sweet is the season of rest,
  When life's weary journey is done!

The blush that spreads over its west,
　　The last lingering ray of its sun!
Though dreary the empire of night,
　　I soon shall emerge from its gloom,
And see immortality's light
　　Arise on the shades of the tomb.

4 Then welcome the last rending sighs,
　　When these aching heart-strings shall break;
When death shall extinguish these eyes,
　　And moisten with dew the pale cheek.
No terror the prospect begets;
　　I am not mortality's slave;
The sunbeam of life as it sets
　　Paints a rainbow of peace on the grave.

140　　　　　L. M.　　　　　*Wallin.*
Christ's Resurrection a Pledge of Ours.

WHEN I the holy grave survey
　　Where once my Savior deigned to lie,
I see fulfilled what prophets say,
　　And all the power of death defy.

2 This empty tomb shall now proclaim
　　How weak the bands of conquered death
Sweet pledge, that all who trust his name
　　Shall rise, and draw immortal breath!

3 [Our Surety, freed, declares us free,
　　For whose offences he was seized:

AND ASCENSION.

In *his* release *our own* we see,
 And shout to view Jehovah pleased.]

4 Jesus, once numbered with the dead,
 Unseals his eyes to sleep no more;
And ever lives their cause to plead,
 For whom the pains of death he bore.

5 Thy risen Lord, my soul, behold!
 See the rich diadem he wears!
Thou, too, shalt bear a harp of gold,
 To crown thy joy when he appears.

6 Though in the dust I lay my head,
 Yet, gracious God, thou wilt not leave
My flesh forever with the dead,
 Nor lose thy children in the grave.

141   C. M.   *Watts.*
Hope of Heaven by the Resurrection of Christ.—
 1 Peter i. 3, 5.

BLEST be the everlasting God.
 The Father of our Lord,
Be his abounding mercy praised,
 His majesty adored.

2 When from the dead he raised his Son,
 And called him to the sky,
He gave our souls a lively hope
 That they should never die.

3 What though our inbred sin requires
    Our flesh to see the dust?
Yet as the Lord our Savior rose,
    So all his followers must.

4 There's an inheritance divine
    Reserved against that day;
'Tis uncorrupted, undefiled,
    And cannot waste away.

5 Saints by the power of God are kept
    Till the salvation come;
We walk by faith as strangers here
    Till Christ shall call us home.

CHRIST'S INTERCESSION.

142   C. M. (Abridged.)   *Toplady.*
Christ's Intercession Prevalent.—John xvii. 24.

AWAKE, sweet gratitude, and sing
    The ascended Savior's love;
Sing how he lives to carry on
    His people's cause above.

2 With cries and tears he offered up
    His humble suit below,
But with authority he asks,
    Enthroned in glory now.

3 For all that come to God by him,
    Salvation he demands;
  Points to their names upon his breast,
    And spreads his wounded hands.

4 His sweet atoning sacrifice
    Gives sanction to his claim;
  "Father, I will that all my saints
    Be with me where I am:

5 "By their salvation, recompense
    The sorrows I endured;
  Just to the merits of thy Son,
    And faithful to thy word."

6 Eternal life, at his request,
    To every saint is given;
  Safety below, and, after death,
    The plenitude of heaven.

143   L. M.   *Steele.*

The Intercession of Christ.—Heb. vii. 25.

HE lives! the great Redeemer lives,
  (What joy the blest assurance gives!)
And now, before his Father, God,
Pleads the full merit of his blood.

2 Repeated crimes awake our fears,
  And Justice, armed with frowns, appears,
  But in the Savior's lovely face
  Sweet mercy smiles, and all is peace.

CHRIST'S INTERCESSION.

3 Hence, then, ye black, despairing thoughts!
Above our fears, above our faults,
His powerful intercessions rise,
And guilt recedes, and terror dies.

4 In every dark, distressful hour,
When sin and Satan join their power,
Let this dear hope repel the dart,—
That Jesus bears us on his heart.

5 Great Advocate, Almighty Friend,
On him our humble hopes depend;
Our cause can never, never fail,
For Jesus pleads, and must prevail.

144   8, 7.
Christ Interceding Above.

JESUS, hail, enthroned in glory,
  There forever to abide;
All the heavenly hosts adore thee,
  Seated at thy Father's side.

2 There for sinners thou art pleading;
    There thou dost our place prepare;
  Ever for us interceding,
    Till in glory we appear.

3 Worship, honor, power, and blessing,
    Thou art worthy to receive;
  Loudest praises, without ceasing,
    Meet it is for us to give.

CHRIST'S INTERCESSION.

145 S. M. (Abridged.) *Watts.*
Christ's Intercession.

WELL, the Redeemer's gone
   To appear before our God,
To sprinkle o'er the flaming throne
   With his atoning blood.

2 No fiery vengeance now,
   Nor burning wrath, comes down;
If Justice call for sinners' blood,
   The Savior shows his own.

3 Before his Father's eye
   Our humble suit he moves,
The Father lays his thunder by,
   And looks, and smiles, and loves.

4 Now may our joyful tongues
   Our Maker's honor sing.
Jesus the Priest receives our songs,
   And bears them to the King.

146 6, 6, 6, 6, 8, 8. *Christ. Psalmist*

ARISE, my soul, arise,
   Shake off thy guilty fears,
The bleeding Sacrifice
   In my behalf appears;
Before the throne my Surety stands,
My name is written on his hands.

CHRIST'S INTERCESSION.

2 He ever lives above,
    For me to intercede;
His all-redeeming love,
    His precious blood, to plead;
His blood atoned on Calvary,
And sprinkles now the throne for me.

3 Five bleeding wounds he bears,
    Received on Calvary;
They pour effectual prayers,
    They strongly speak for me;
"Forgive him, oh forgive," they cry
"Nor let that ransomed sinner die!"

4 The Father hears him pray,
    His dear anointed One:
He cannot turn away
    The presence of his Son:
His spirit answers to the blood,
And tells me I am born of God.

5 To God I'm reconciled,
    His pardoning voice I hear:
He owns me for his child,
    I can no longer fear:
With confidence I now draw nigh,
And Father, Abba Father, cry.

UNION WITH CHRIST.

147   L. M.   *Kent.*
Union with Jesus.

'TWIXT Jesus and the chosen race,
  Subsists a bond of sovereign grace,
That hell, with its infernal train,
Shall ne'er dissolve, or rend in twain.

2 This sacred bond shall never break,
Though earth should to her center shake;
Rest, doubting saint, assured of this,
For God has pledged his holiness.

3 He swore but once, the deed was done,
'Twas settled by the great Three One;
Christ was appointed to redeem
All that the Father loved in him.

4 Hail sacred union, firm and strong!
How great the grace, how sweet the song!
That worms of earth should ever be
One with incarnate deity!

5 One in the tomb, one when he rose,
One when he triumphed o'er his foes,
One when in heaven he took his seat,
While seraphs sung all hell's defeat.

6 This sacred tie forbids their fears,
  For all he is, or has, is theirs;
  With him their head, they stand or fall,
  Their life their surety, and their all.

148 S. M. *Kent.*
Ye are all one in Christ.

IN union with the Lamb,
  From condemnation free,
The saints from everlasting were,
  And shall forever be.

2 In covenant from of old,
    The sons of God they were;
  The feeblest lamb in Jesus' fold
    Was blessed in Jesus there.

3 Its bonds shall never break,
    Though earth's old column's bow;
  The strong, the tempted, and the weak,
    Are one in Jesus now.

4 With joy lift up your heads,
    Ye highly favored few—
  When through the earth destruction spreads,
    For what shall injure you?

5 When storms or tempests rise,
    Or sins your peace assail,
  Your hope in Jesus never dies—
    'Tis cast within the veil.

6 Here let the weary rest,
   Who love the Savior's name;
 Though with no sweet enjoyment blest,
   This covenant stands the same.

149   7s.   *Cennick*

Rejoicing in Hope.—Isa. xxxv. 10—Luke xii. 32.

CHILDREN of the heavenly King,
   As you journey sweetly sing;
 Sing your Savior's worthy praise,
 Glorious in his works and ways.

2 Ye are traveling home to God,
 In the way the fathers trod;
 They are happy now, and ye
 Soon their happiness shall see.

3 O, ye banished seed, be glad!
 Christ our Advocate is made;
 Us, to save, our flesh assumes,
 Brother to our souls becomes.

4 Shout, ye little flock, and blest!
 You on Jesus' throne shall rest;
 There your seat is now prepared—
 There your kingdom and reward.

5 Fear not, brethren, joyful stand
 On the borders of your land;
 Christ, your Father's elder Son,
 Bids you undismayed go on

6 Lord! submissive make us go,
   Gladly leaving all below;
   Only thou our Leader be,
   And we still will follow thee.

150   L. M.   *Vanmeter.*
Union with Christ.

A SACRED union we behold;
   Christ and his people all allied;
He the great Shepherd of the fold,
   And they the sheep for whom he died.

2 When they, like sheep had gone estray,
   Their sins were laid upon his head;
He gave his life their debts to pay,
   And for their breach atonement made.

3 He is their Father, they his sons,
   Bound by indissoluble ties;
All of his flesh and of his bones,
   And heirs to mansions in the skies.

4 He is the Husband, and his love,
   Has been eternal toward his bride;
Nor will his strong affections move,
   Until he seats her by his side.

5 She was insolvent, and he paid
   The utmost farthing that she owed;
She was in filthy rags arrayed,
   And he a spotless robe bestowed.

Unite us gracious Lord, to thee,
   By love and by a living faith;
Till we have crossed this boisterous sea,
   And moored beyond the gates of death.

51   S. M.   *Doddridge.*
Vital Union to Christ in Regeneration.—1 Cor. vi. 17.

DEAR Savior, we are thine,
   By everlasting bonds;
Our names, our hearts, we would resign,
   Our souls are in thy hands.

To thee we still would cleave
   With ever-growing zeal;
If millions tempt us Christ to leave,
   O let them ne'er prevail.

Death may our souls divide
   From these abodes of clay;
But love shall keep us near thy side
   Through all the gloomy way.

Since Christ and we are one,
   Why should we doubt or fear?
If he in heaven hath fixed his throne,
   He'll fix his members there.

52   7s.   *Sonnets.*
Christ Presenting the Saints to the Father.

'TIS the Bridegroom's voice I hear,
   With his bride divinely fair,
Standing round Jehovah's throne,
Crowned with glory, lacking none.

2 "Here am I, and those with me,
   Zion's numerous progeny;
   Fruit of all the pains I bore;
   Counted with precision o'er.

3 "None I've lost of all the race
   Called a remnant saved by grace;
   None of heaven miscarried yet,
   Bought by Calvary's bloody sweat.

4 "Objects of eternal care,
   By creation thine they were;
   Chosen sheep within thy fold,
   Ransomed from the days of old.

5 "Thine by renovating grace,
   Thine in love and faithfulness;
   Safely kept by grace divine,
   In eternal wedlock mine.

6 "Thine they were, when dead in sin,
   Slaves to every lust obscene;
   With their Maker's ways at war,
   Far from God, yea, very far.

7 "Thine in counsel and decree;
   Loved with love beyond degree,
   Long before their father's fall,
   Blest in Jesus, one and all.

8 "Thine by all the sacred ties,
   Solemn oaths and promises,
   God could give, or men receive,
   Hope expect, or faith believe."

PREDESTINATION AND ELECTION.

153　　　　L. M.　　　　*Watts.*

Electing Grace; or, Saints Beloved in Christ.
　　　—Eph. i. 3, etc.

JESUS, we bless thy Father's name;
　Thy God and ours are both the same;
What heavenly blessings from his throne
Flow down to sinners through his Son!

2 "Christ be my first elect," he said,
Then chose our souls in Christ our Head,
Before he gave the mountains birth,
Or laid foundations for the earth.

3 Thus did eternal love begin
To raise us up from death and sin;
Our characters were then decreed,
"Blameless in love, a holy seed.

4 Predestinated to be sons,
Born by degrees, but chose at once;
A new regenerated race
To praise the glories of his grace.

5 With Christ our Lord we share a part
In the affections of his heart;
Nor shall our souls be thence removed
Till he forgets his first beloved.

154   L. M.   *Tucke.*
Union with Christ.—2 Tim. 1. 9.

EXPAND, my soul, arise and sing
The matchless grace of Sion's King;
Whose love, as ancient as his name,
Let all thy powers aloud proclaim.

2 'Twas he, eternal ages past,
Formed his great plan from first to last;
And what his arm would e'er fulfill
Stood ever present to his will.

3 He saw, with one capacious glance,
World upon world to life advance,
And fixed the end, ere time began,
Of seraph, reptile, and of man.

4 Of man, chief work of all below,
What wonders are we led to know!
Wonders surpassing angels' thought
Are by our God in Jesus taught.

5 Grace, deep as the Eternal Mind,
Unutterable bliss designed
For man, ere worlds or sin were born,
Or angels sang creations's morn.

6 Chosen of old, of old approved;
In Christ, the eternal Son, beloved;
Adopted too, and children made,
Ere sin its baneful poison spread.

155   L. M.   *Vanmeter.*
Chosen in Christ.

ETERNAL, ere the worlds were made,
   Were all God's purposes of Grace;
Nought can disturb the plan he laid
   To glorify his chosen race.

2 His first elect was Christ, his Son;
   In him he chose his numerous seed;
They were in bondage and undone,
   But lo! he dies and they are freed.

3 To recompense his dying groans,
   He gave him all for whom he died;
Engaged the honors of his throne,
   To seat his favorites at his side.

4 And now he sends his Spirit down,
   To fit them for the blest abode;
To make his covenant mercies known,
   And guide them on the heavenly road.

5 He fixed their first and second birth;
   Ordained the manner, time and place;
Their joys and sorrows here on earth,
   Their cups of grief and sweets of grace.

6 O, may my warmest passions move,
   That such a worthless worm as I,
Should be an object of his love,
   And taste of such a sacred joy!

PREDESTINATION.

156 C. M. *Presby. Selec.*
Summary of Doctrines.

LET me, my Savior and my God,
 On sovereign grace rely;
And own 'tis free, because bestowed
 On one so vile as I.

2 Election! 'tis a word divine;
 For, Lord, I plainly see,
Had not thy choice prevented mine,
 I ne'er had chosen thee.

3 For perseverance, strength, I've none,
 But would on this depend,
That Jesus, having loved his own,
 Will love them to the end.

4 Empty and bare, I come to thee
 For righteousness divine:
Oh, may thy glorious merits be
 By imputation mine!

5 Free grace alone can wipe the tears
 From my lamenting eyes,
And raise my soul, from guilty fears,
 To joy that never dies.

6 Free grace can death itself outbrave,
 And take the sting away;
Can sinners to the utmost save,
 And give them victory.

157   7s. (Abridged.)   *Ryland.*
Decrees of God.—Ps. xxxi. 15.

SOVEREIGN Ruler of the skies!
Ever gracious, ever wise!
All my times are in thy hand,
All events at thy command.

2 His decree, who formed the earth,
Fixed my first and second birth;
Parents, native place, and time,
All appointed were by him.

3 He that formed me in the womb,
He shall guide me to the tomb;
All my times shall ever be
Ordered by his wise decree.

4 Times of sickness, times of health,
Times of penury and wealth,
Times of trial and of grief;
Times of triumph and relief:

5 Times the tempter's power to prove;
Times to taste a Savior's love;
All must come, and last, and end,
As shall please my heavenly Friend.

6 Plagues and deaths around me fly;
Till he bid, I cannot die;
Not a single shaft can hit
Till the God of love sees fit.

7 O thou Gracious, Wise, and Just,
   In thy hands my life I trust;
   Have I somewhat dearer still?
   I resign it to thy will.

158   C. M.   *Watts.*
The Book of God's Decrees.

LET the whole race of creatures lie
   Abased before their God;
Whate'er his sovereign voice hath formed
   He governs with a nod.

2 [Ten thousand ages ere the skies
   Were into motion brought,
All the long years and worlds to come
   Stood present to his thought.

3 There's not a sparrow or a worm,
   But's found in his decrees;
He raises monarchs to their thrones,
   And sinks them as he please.]

4 If light attend the course I run,
   'Tis he provides those rays:
And 'tis his hand that hides my sun,
   If darkness clouds my days.

5 Yet I would not be much concerned,
   Nor vainly long, to see

The volume of his deep decrees,
  What months are writ for me.

6 When he reveals the book of life,
   Oh, may I read my name
  Among the chosen of his love,
   The followers of the Lamb!

159　　　　　L. M.　　　　*Burnham.*
Decrees of God.—Eph. i. 11.

'TWAS fixed in God's eternal mind,
  When his dear sons should mercy find;
From everlasting he decreed
When every good should be conveyed.

2 Determined was the manner how
  We should be brought the Lord to know;
  Yea, he decreed the very place
  Where he would call us by his grace.

3 [Vast were the settlements of grace
  On millions of the human race;
  And every favor richly given
  Flows from the high decrees of heaven.

4 In every mercy, full and free,
  The appointing God I wish to see;
  To see how grace, free grace, has reigned
  In every blessing he ordained.

5 Yes, dearest Lord, 'tis my desire
  Thy wise appointments to admire,
  And trace the footsteps of my God
  Through every part of Zion's road.

160   L. M.   *Kent.*

Predestination to Eternal Life made known by Calling.

THERE is a period known to God,
When all his sheep redeemed by blood,
Shall leave the hateful ways of sin,
Turn to the fold and enter in.

2 At peace with hell, with God at war,
In sin's dark maze they wander far;
Indulge their lust, and still go on
As far from God as sheep can run.

3 But see how Heaven's indulgent care
Attends their wanderings here and there:
Still hard at heel, where'er they stray,
With piercing thorns to hedge their way.

4 When wisdom calls they stop their ear,
And headlong urge the mad career;
Judgments nor mercies ne'er can sway
Their roving feet to wisdom's way.

5 Glory to God, they ne'er shall rove
Beyond the limits of his love;
Fenced with Jehovah's *shalls* and *wills*,
Firm as the everlasting hills.

6 The appointed time rolls on apace,
Not to *propose*, but *call* by grace;
To change the heart, renew the will,
And turn the feet to Zion's hill.

161   C. M.   *Watts.*

Election Excludes Boasting.—1 Cor. i. 26, 31.

BUT few among the carnal wise,
    But few of noble race,
Obtain the favor of thine eyes,
    Almighty King of grace.

2 He takes the men of meanest name
    For sons and heirs of God ;
And thus he pours abundant shame
    On honorable blood.

3 He calls the fool, and makes him know
    The mysteries of his grace,
To bring aspiring wisdom low,
    And all its pride abase.

4 Nature has all its glories lost
    When brought before his throne:
No flesh shall in his presence boast,
    But in the Lord alone.

SALVATION AND REDEMPTION.

162   L. M.   *Steele.*

Redemption by Christ alone.—1 Peter i. 18, 19.

ENSLAVED by sin, and bound in chains
    Beneath its dreadful tyrant sway,
And doomed to everlasting pains,
    We wretched, guilty captives lay.

2 Nor gold nor gems could buy our peace,
 Nor the whole world's collected store
Suffice to purchase our release—
 A thousand worlds were all too poor.

3 Jesus, the Lord, the mighty God,
 An all-sufficient ransom paid:
Invalued price! his precious blood
 For vile, rebellious traitors shed.

4 Jesus the sacrifice became
 To rescue guilty souls from hell;
The spotless, bleeding, dying Lamb
 Beneath avenging justice fell.

5 Amazing goodness! love divine!
 Oh, may our grateful hearts adore
The matchless grace, nor yield to sin,
 Nor wear its cruel fetters more!

6 Dear Savior, let thy love pursue
 The glorious work it has begun;
Each secret, lurking foe subdue,
 And let our hearts be thine alone.

163 7s. (Abridged.) *Rippon's Selec.*

Redeeming Love.

NOW begin the heavenly theme,
 Sing aloud in Jesus' name!
Ye who his salvation prove,
Triumph in redeeming love.

2 Ye who see the Father's grace
　Beaming in the Savior's face,
　As to Canaan on ye move,
　Praise and bless redeeming love.

3 Mourning souls, dry up your tears:
　Banish all your guilty fears;
　See your guilt and curse remove,
　Cancelled by redeeming love.

4 Ye, alas! who long have been
　Willing slaves to death and sin,
　Now from bliss no longer rove,
　Stop and taste redeeming love.

5 Welcome, all by sin opprest,
　Welcome to his sacred rest:
　Nothing brought him from above,
　Nothing but redeeming love.

6 When the Spirit leads us home,
　When we to his glory come,
　We shall all the fullness prove
　Of our Lord's redeeming love.

164　　　　L. M.　　　　*Vanmeter.*
　　　　Redemption.

REDEMPTION! O, the joyful news!
　To Gentile nations and to Jews:
What consolation it imparts,
To mourning souls and broken hearts!

2 In bondage and in prison bound,
  No peace nor pardon could be found,
  Till this redemption was revealed,
  And by the blood of Jesus sealed.

3 Redeemed from justice by his blood,
  And from the righteous laws of God;
  O'er sin and Satan we'll proclaim
  Redemption through the Savior's name.

4 Soon shall the saints of every place,
  Be joined to sing redeeming grace;
  And every kindred, every tongue,
  Shall add its music to the song.

165 C. M. *Watts.*
Redemption by Price and Power.

JESUS, with all thy saints above,
  My tongue would bear her part,
Would sound aloud thy saving love
  And sing thy bleeding heart.

2 Blessed be the Lamb, my dearest Lord,
  Who bought me with his blood,
  And quenched his Father's flaming sword
  In his own vital flood;

3 The Lamb that freed my captive soul
  From Satan's heavy chains,
  And sent the lion down to howl
  Where hell and horror reigns.

4 All glory to the dying Lamb,
  And never-ceasing praise,
While angels live to know his name
  Or saints to feel his grace.

166 L. M. *Vanmeter.*
Salvation.

SALVATION! what a heavenly theme!
Salvation free through Jesus' name!
Let all the saints in concert join,
To sing salvation so divine.

2 Bound by the chains of sin, we lie
As rebels, justly doomed to die,
Till this salvation sounds release,
And bids us prisoners go in peace.

3 Salvation like a river flows,
With healing balm for all our woes;
Its heavenly streams which flow abroad,
Make glad the city of our God.

4 Saved from the regions of despair,
And from ten thousand dangers here;
From doubts, and fears, and every foe;
We'll sing salvation as we go.

5 Salvation! O, that we may sing
Salvation from the monster's sting!
And o'er the grave a victory gain,
And with King Jesus ever reign.

167   C. M.   *Kent.*

The Lamb and his Virgin Company.

ON Zion's sacred mount I saw
    The Lamb for sinners slain;
His church, redeemed from endless woe,
    Composed his glorious train.

2 This virgin throng, beloved of God,
    All stood around him there,
With garments washed in his own blood,
    Divinely bright and fair.

3 I strove this blood-bought host to count,
    Thus to my sight revealed;
And found at last their full amount:
    'Twas all that God had sealed.

4 They sung a song forever new,
    And none could learn the same
But ransomed slaves and sinners who
    From tribulation came.

5 They hymned the great, the dread I AM
    Whose sacred name they wore,
With endless honors to the Lamb
    Till time shall be no more.

6 Blameless before his throne they stand;
    They make a joyful noise,—
A called, a faithful, chosen band,—
    And vent their swelling joys.

168   L. M.   *Kent.*

Salvation by Grace.

GOD, in the riches of his grace,
   Did from eternity ordain
A seed elect, of Adam's race,
   Eternal glory should obtain.

2 God, in the riches of his grace
   Hath Christ exalted over all;
His goings forth of old we trace,
   The sinner's surety in the fall.

3 God, in the riches of his grace,
   Hath Abram's seed exalted high,
While sinning angels, from his face,
   Reserved to wrath, in fetters lie.

4 God, in the riches of his grace,
   Hath to the charge of Jesus laid
The sin of all that chosen race,
   Whose debt of suffering Jesus paid.

5 God, in the riches of his grace,
   Hath in the gospel Christ **displayed**,
Whose blood hath sealed **the sinner's** peace
   And bruised the envenomed serpent's head.

6 God, in the riches of his grace,
   We'll to eternity adore,
And wonders still on wonders trace,
   But ne'er this depth of love explore.

169   L. M.   *Vunmet*
Free Grace.

'TIS grace, free grace, eternal grace!
Deserves our highest songs of praise;
We'll join and sing with hearts and tongues,
With grace the burden of our songs.

2 'Twas grace that found a rebel lost,
And brought him back, tho' great the cost:
Took off his rags, and in their place,
Gave him a robe of righteousness.

3 This costly robe's without a seam,
And hides my guilt, and sin, and shame;
'Twas on a worthless worm bestowed,
The gift of God through Jesus' blood.

4 Grace brings the haughty monarch down,
Exalts the beggar to a crown;
Makes hills and mountains melt away,
And valleys rise as high as they.

5 This grace is all the Christian's boast;
This is his hope, his joy, his trust;
Free grace alone, from first to last,
Directs his way and holds him fast.

6 While I have breath this grace shall be
My only theme, my only plea;
And may I, when this body dies,
Sing sovereign grace above the skies.

70   8s.   *Chappell.*

Salvation.—Acts iv. 12.

SALVATION, how precious the sound
  To sinners who see themselves lost;
To Jesus their praises redound,
  In Jesus they triumph and boast.

Salvation is finished and done,
  Salvation is sovereign and free;
Salvation by God's equal Son
  My joy and rejoicing shall be.

Salvation is only of God,
  To him all the praises are due;
Ye saints, spread his honors abroad,
  Who finished salvation for you.

Soon shall we behold him above,
  Forever to sound his dear name;
To sing the sweet song of his love,
  Salvation to God and the Lamb!

71   L. M.   *Watts.*

Christ and his Righteousness.—Phil. iii. 7–9.

NO more, my God, I boast no more
  Of all the duties I have done;
I quit the hopes I held before,
  To trust the merits of thy Son.

Now, for the love I bear his name,
  What was my gain I count my loss,

SALVATION

My former pride I call my shame,
  And nail my glory to his cross.

3 Yes, and I must and will esteem
  All things but loss for Jesus' sake:
Oh, may my soul be found in him,
  And of his righteousness partake.

4 The best obedience of my hands
  Dares not appear before thy throne;
But faith can answer thy demands,
  By pleading what my Lord has done.

172   C. M.   *Kent.*
Everlasting Love.

BENEATH the sacred throne of God
  I saw a river rise,
The streams were peace, and pardoning blood,
  Descending from the skies.

2 Angelic minds cannot explore
  This deep, unfathomed sea;
'Tis void of bottom, brim, or shore,
  And lost in Deity.

3 I stood amazed, and wondered when
  Or why this ocean rose,
That wafts salvation down to men,
  His traitors and his foes.

4 That sacred flood, from Jesus' veins,
  Was free to take away
A Mary's or Manasseh's stains,
  Or sins more vile than they:

5 Free to the sinner dead to God,
    Who sought the road to hell,
That trampled on a Savior's blood,
    And on his buckler fell.

6 Triumphant grace, and man's free will,
    Shall not divide the throne;
For man's a fallen sinner still,
    And Christ shall reign alone.

173   S. M.   *Watts.*
Salvation by Grace, from first to last—Eph. ii. 5.

GRACE! 'tis a charming sound!
    Harmonious to the ear!
Heaven with the echo shall resound,
    And all the earth shall hear.

2 Grace first contrived the way
    To save rebellious man;
And all the steps *that* grace display
    Which drew the wondrous plan.

3 [Grace first inscribed my name
    In God's eternal book;
'Twas grace that gave me to the Lamb,
    Who all my sorrows took.]

4 Grace led my roving feet
    To tread the heavenly road;
And new supplies, each hour, I meet,
    While pressing on to God.

5 [Grace taught my soul to pray,
    And made my eyes o'erflow;
'Twas grace which kept me to this day,
    And will not let me go.]

6 Grace all the work shall crown,
    Through everlasting days;
It lays in heaven the topmost stone,
    And well deserves the praise.

174   C. M.   *Rippon's Selec.*
By the Grace of God, I am what I am.—1 Cor. xv. 8.

GREAT God, 'tis from thy sovereign grace
    That all my blessings flow;
Whate'er I am, or do possess,
    I to thy mercy owe.

2 'Tis this my powerful lust controls,
    And pardons all my sin;
Spreads life and comfort through my soul,
    And makes my nature clean.

3 'Tis this upholds me whilst I live,
    Supports me when I die;
And hence ten thousand saints receive
    Their all, as well as I.

4 How full must be the springs from whence
    Such various streams proceed!
The pasture cannot but be rich
    On which so many feed.

JUSTIFICATION.

175 S. M. *Watts.*
Dead to Sin by the Cross of Christ.

SHALL we go on to sin
  Because thy grace abounds,
Or crucify the Lord again,
  And open all his wounds?

2 Forbid it, mighty God,
  Nor let it e'er be said
That we whose sins are crucified
  Should raise them from the dead.

3 We will be slaves no more,
  Since Christ has made us free,
Has nailed our tyrants to his cross,
  And bought our liberty.

JUSTIFICATION.

176 C. M. *Watts.*
Justification by Faith, not by Works; or, the Law Condemns, Grace Justifies. —Rom. iii. 19, 22.

VAIN are the hopes that sons of men
  On their own works have built;
Their hearts by nature all unclean,
  And all their actions guilt.

2 Let Jews and Gentiles stop their mouths,
  Without a murmuring word,

JUSTIFICATION.

And the whole race of Adam stand
   Guilty before the Lord.

3 In vain we ask God's righteous law
     To justify us now,
  Since to convince and to condemn
     Is all the law can do.

4 Jesus, how glorious is thy grace!
     When in thy name we trust,
  Our faith receives a righteousness
     That makes the sinner just.

177   L. M.   *Watts.*
Imputed Righteousness.—Jer. xxiii. 6; Isa. xlv. 24.

JESUS, thy blood and righteousness
   My beauty are, my glorious dress;
Midst flaming worlds, in these arrayed,
With joy shall I lift up my head.

2 When from the dust of death I rise
  To take my mansion in the skies,
  E'en then shall this be all my plea:
  "Jesus hath lived and died for me."

3 Bold shall I stand in that great day,
  For who aught to my charge shall lay?
  While through thy blood absolved I am
  From sin's tremendous curse and shame.

4 Thus Abraham, the friend of God,
  Thus all the armies bought with blood,

Savior of sinners, thee proclaim!
Sinners,—of whom the chief I am.

5 This spotless robe the same appears
When ruined nature sinks in years;
No age can change its glorious hue:
The robe of Christ is ever new.

6 Oh, let the dead now hear thy voice!
Bid, Lord, thy banished ones rejoice;
Their beauty this, their glorious dress,
Jesus, the Lord, our righteousness.

178 L. M. *Vanmeter.*
Imputed Righteousness.

I AM a miracle of grace!
　Snatched from the regions of despair:
My feet had well nigh reached the place,
　When Jesus stopped my wild career.

2 Against him long I had rebelled,
　And vanity was my delight;
But when my danger I beheld,
　I stood and trembled at the sight!

3 To venture on, I saw would be,
　My everlasting overthrow;
To turn, would meet the Deity,
　With awful vengeance on his brow.

4 Death seemed to stand on every side,
　Yet I resolved my death to meet,
[Where one before had never died—]
　Imploring mercy at his feet.

JUSTIFICATION.

5 But strange to tell, he bade me live!
    Just in the last extremity,
He smiled and said "I all forgive;
    Believe, and thou shalt never die."

6 With joy, ineffable, I saw
    That justice had been satisfied
In Christ, who had fulfilled the law,
    And for his people bled and died.

7 "Thy sins were laid upon my Son,"
    In accents sweet, the Father said:
"His righteousness is now thy own,
    Thou art his member, he thy Head.'

8 Not all the outward forms of men,
    Can with this righteousness compare;
It makes the guilty conscience clean,
    Nor leaves a spot or blemish there.

179   L. M.   *Kent.*

Justification by the Imputed Righteousness of Christ.

BEFORE the covenant angel's face,
    See Joshua stands in vile array,
Deep run in debt, a dreadful case!
    Unable one small mite to pay.

2 Weighed in the balance, found too light,
    He hides his face, nor dares reply;
Justice uplifts her sword to smite—
    But must the trembling sinner die?

3 Hear Jesus speak, while from his eyes
    Immortal love and pity beam :
  Take from him all his filthy guise,
    And place my spotless robe on him.

4 Now, Justice, view the law-cursed wretch,
    If aught deficient thou canst see,
  But let thy hand forbear to touch—
    That sinner's justified by me.

5 For him I bore the dreadful smart
    Of hell's more dire eternal pain ;
  Let this suffice, or through my heart
    Thrust thy dread weapon once again.

6 Go, then, and to the law's demands,
    Plead what thy suffering Lord has done ;
  Weep o'er thy sins that pierced his hands
    And trust in his free grace alone.

180   C. M.   *Kent.*
Insolvent Debtors Clad in the Righteousness of Christ, Justified from all Things.

JESUS hath magnified the law,
  Hath banished hell and sin ;
And righteousness without a flaw
  Brought once forever in.

2 Insolvents clad in this array,
    Fear not Mount Sinai's din ;
  'Twill stand when earth shall pass away ;
    'Twas brought by Jesus in.

JUSTIFICATION.

3 This change of raiment ye possess,
    Is linen white and clean;
  'Tis called "Jehovah's righteousness;"
    'Twas brought by Jesus in.

4 Zion shall make her boast of this,
    And life eternal win;
  'Tis everlasting righteousness;
    'Twas brought by Jesus in.

5 This royal robe, this wedding dress,
    Shall cancel all our sin,
  Of crimes, the greater and the less;
    'Twas brought by Jesus in.

6 This only robe shall God approve,
    To hide thy stains of sin;
  'Twas wove by everlasting love,
    And brought by Jesus in.

181   L. M.   *Vanmeter.*
Justification through Christ.

HOW can a sinner stand before
  A God of holiness and power?
What kind of robe can he provide,
His guilt and nakedness to hide?

2 Though he to Sinai's mountain flies,
  There justice stands with flaming eyes;
  And pours its curses on his head,
  And bids him fly, or dooms him dead.

JUSTIFICATION. 167

3 Amazed, the sinner next repairs,
And seeks a shelter 'neath his prayers;
But justice finds his hiding place.
And there presents his fiery face.

4 The sinner now almost despairs;
He's tried the law, and tried his prayers;
He's tried morality in vain,
And feels his load of guilt remain.

5 But, midst his consternation, he
Beholds one hanging on a tree;
And justice pours upon his head,
Its vengeance, in the sinner's stead!

6 Yes, Jesus bears the heavy load,
And stays the justice of a God!
The righteousness of Christ appears.
And is the robe the sinner wears.

182 C. M. *Watts.*
The Robe of Righteousness and Garments of Salvation —Isa. lxi. 10.

AWAKE, my heart, arise, my tongue,
  Prepare a tuneful voice;
In God, the life of all my joys,
  Aloud will I rejoice.

2 'Tis he adorned my naked soul,
  And made salvation mine;
Upon a poor, polluted worm
  He makes his graces shine.

3 And, lest the shadow of a spot
  Should on my soul be found,
 He took the robe the Savior wrought,
  And cast it all around.

4 How far the heavenly robe exceeds
  What earthly princes wear;
 These ornaments, how bright they shine;
  How white the garments are.

5 The Spirit wrought my faith, and love,
  And hope, and every grace;
 But Jesus spent his life to work
  The robe of righteousness.

6 Strangely, my soul, art thou arrayed
  By the great sacred Three;
 In sweetest harmony of praise
  Let all thy powers agree.

FORGIVENESS AND PARDON.

183 C. M. *Parkinson's Selec.*
  Remember me.

JESUS, thou art the sinner's friend;
  As such I look to thee;
Now in the bowels of thy love,
  O Lord, remember me.

2 Remember thy pure word of grace,
   Remember Calvary;
Remember all thy dying groans,
   And then remember me.

3 Thou wondrous advocate with God,
   I yield myself to thee;
While thou art sitting on thy throne,
   Dear Lord, remember me.

4 I own I'm guilty, own I'm vile,
   Yet thy salvation 's free;
Then in thy all-abounding grace,
   Dear Lord, remember me.

5 Howe'er forsaken or distressed,
   Howe'er oppressed I be,
Howe'er afflicted here on earth,
   Do thou remember me.

6 And when I close my eyes in death,
   And creature-helps all flee,
Then O, my dear Redeemer, God,
   I pray remember me.

184   L. M.   *Gibbons.*

Thy sins are Forgiven thee.—Luke vii. 47, 48.

FORGIVENESS! 'tis a joyful sound
   To malefactors doomed to die:
Publish the bliss the world around,
   Ye seraphs, shout it from the sky!

2 'Tis the rich gift of love divine;
    'Tis full, outmeasuring every crime:
Unclouded shall its glories shine,
    And feel no change by changing time.

3 O'er sins unnumbered as the sand,
    And like the mountains for their size,
The seas of sovereign grace expand,
    The seas of sovereign grace arise.

4 For this stupendous love of heaven
    What grateful honors shall we show?
Where much transgression is forgiven,
    Let love in equal ardor glow.

185 C. M. *Doddridge.*

Pardon Spoken by Christ.—Matt. ix. 2.

MY Savior, let me hear thy voice
    Pronounce the words of peace,
And all my warmest powers shall join
    To celebrate thy grace.

2 With gentle smiles call me thy child,
    And speak my sins forgiven;
The accents mild shall charm mine ear,
    All like the harps of heaven.

3 Cheerful, where'er thy hand shall lead,
    The darkest path I'll tread;
Cheerful I'll quit these mortal shores,
    And mingle with the dead.

FORGIVENESS AND PARDON.

4 When dreadful guilt is done away,
   No other fears we know;
That hand which scatters pardons down
   Shall crowns of life bestow.

186 C. M. *Watts, (altered.)*
Pardon and Sanctification in Christ.

IS there no shelter from the wrath
   Of an offended God?
Jesus, to thy dear cross I fly,
   Thy sin-atoning blood.

2 I bless that stream that cries for peace
   From every bleeding vein;
Yet is my soul but half redeemed,
   If sin, the tyrant, reign.

3 Lord, crush his empire, bid his throne
   From its foundation fall;
Ye flattering plagues, that wrought my death,
   Fly, for I hate you all.

4 Now to the Lamb, whose power and grace
   Lift our bright hopes to heaven,
In songs above, and songs below,
   Be endless glory given.

187 C. M. *Steele.*
Pardoning Love.—Jer. iii. 22; Hos. xiv. 4.

HOW oft, alas! this wretched heart
   Has wandered from the Lord!

FORGIVENESS AND PARDON.

How oft my roving thoughts depart,
  Forgetful of his word!

2 Yet sovereign mercy calls, "Return;"
  Dear Lord, and may I come!
My vile ingratitude I mourn:
  Oh, take the wanderer home!

3 And canst thou, wilt thou, yet forgive,
  And bid my crimes remove?
And shall a pardoned rebel live
  To speak thy wondrous love?

4 Almighty grace, thy healing power,
  How glorious, how divine!
That can to life and bliss restore
  So vile a heart as mine.

5 Thy pardoning love, so free, so sweet·
  Dear Savior, I adore;
Oh, keep me at thy sacred feet,
  And let me rove no more!

188   S. M.   *Watts.*

Confession and Pardon.—1 John i. 9; Prov. xxviii. 13.

MY sorrows, like a flood,
  Impatient of restraint,
Into thy bosom, O, my God,
  Pour out a long complaint.

2 This impious heart of mine
  Could once defy the Lord,

Could rush with violence on to sin
 In presence of thy sword.

3 How often have I stood
 A rebel to the skies!
And yet, and yet—oh, matchless grace!—
 Thy thunder silent lies.

4 Oh, shall I never feel
 The meltings of thy love?
Am I of such hell-hardened steel
 That mercy cannot move?

5 O'ercome by dying love,
 Here at thy cross I lie,
And throw my flesh, my soul, my all,
 And weep, and love, and die.

6 "Rise," says the Savior, "rise!
 Behold my wounded veins!
Here flows a sacred crimson flood
 To wash away thy stains."

7 See, God is reconciled!
 Behold his smiling face!
Let joyful cherubs clap their wings,
 And sound aloud his grace.

REGENERATION AND CONVERSION.

189   C. M.   *Hoskins.*

Ye must be born again.—John iii. 7.

SINNERS! this solemn truth regard!
   Hear, all ye sons of men;
For Christ the Savior hath declared,
   "Ye must be born again."

2 Whate'er might be your birth or blood,
   The sinner's boast is vain:
Thus saith the glorious Son of God:
   "Ye must be born again."

3 Our nature totally depraved,
   The heart a sink of sin,
Without a change we can't be saved,
   "We must be born again."

4 That which is born of flesh is flesh,
   And flesh it will remain;
Then marvel not that Jesus saith,
   "Ye must be born again."

5 Spirit of life! thy grace impart,
   And breathe on sinners slain;
And witness, Lord, in every heart,
   That we are born again.

6 [Dear Savior, let us now begin
  To trust and love thy word;
And by forsaking every sin,
  Prove we are born of God.]

190 8, 8, 6. *Kent's Selec*

Necessity of Regeneration.

AWAKED by Sinai's awful sound,
  My soul in bonds of guilt I found,
    And knew not where to go;
O'erwhelmed with sin, with anguish slain,
The sinner must be BORN AGAIN,
    Or sink to endless woe.

2 Amazed I stood, but could not tell
  Which way to shun the gates of hell,
    For death and hell drew near;
I strove indeed, but strove in vain;
The sinner must be BORN AGAIN,
    Still sounded in my ear.

3 Then to the law I trembling fled,
  It poured its curses on my head,
    I no relief could find;
This fearful truth increased my pain,
The sinner must be BORN AGAIN,
    O'erwhelmed my tortured mind.

4 Again did Sinai's thunders roll,
  And guilt lay heavy on my soul,
    A vast, unwieldy load;
Alas! I read and saw it plain,

REGENERATION

The sinner must be BORN AGAIN,
    Or drink the wrath of God.

5 The saints I heard with rapture tell
    How Jesus conquered death and hell
        And broke the fowler's snare;
    Yet, when I found this truth remain,
The sinner must be BORN AGAIN,
        I sank in deep despair.

6 But while I thus in anguish lay,
    Jesus of Nazareth passed that way,
        And felt his pity move;
    The sinner, by his justice slain,
    Now, by his grace, is BORN AGAIN,
        And sings redeeming love.

191　　　　　C. M.　　*Watts, (altered.)*
Regeneration.—John i. 13.

NOT all the outward forms on earth,
    Nor rites that God has given,
Nor will of man, nor blood, nor birth,
    Can raise a soul to heaven.

2 The sovereign will of God alone
    Creates us heirs of grace;
Born in the image of his Son,
    A new, peculiar race.

3 The Spirit, like some heavenly wind,
    Blows on the sons of flesh,
Renews the spirit of the mind,
    And forms the man afresh.

4 Our quickened souls awake, and rise
   From the long sleep of death;
On heavenly things we fix our eyes,
   And praise employs our breath.

192   8s, 7s.   *Swain.*
Praise for Conversion.—Jer. xxxi. 3.

ON the brink of fiery ruin,
   Justice, with a flaming sword,
Was my guilty soul pursuing,
   When I first beheld my Lord.

2 [Terrified with Sinai's thunder,
   Straight I flew to Calvary:
Where I saw with love and wonder
   Him, by faith, who died for me.]

3 "Sinner," he exclaimed, "I've loved thee
   With an everlasting love;
Justice has in me approved thee;
   Thou shalt dwell with me above."

4 Sweet as angels' notes in heaven,
   When to golden harps they sound,
Is the voice of sins forgiven
   To the soul by Satan bound.

5 Sweet as angels' harp in glory
   Was that heavenly voice to me,
When I saw my Lord before me,
   Bleed and die to set me free!

6 Saints, attend with holy wonder!
    Sinners, hear and sing his praise!
'Tis the God that holds the thunder
    Shows himself the God of grace.

193   7s.   *Vanmeter.*

The Stranger.

STRANGER, if thou want to know,
    Who I am, and how I do,
Come and listen while I tell
Who I am, and where I dwell:

2 I was lost in nature's night;
    Without hearing, without sight;
Faint with sickness, wounded, sore,
Deep in debt, and very poor.

3 Jesus found me in this state,
    Kindly canceled all my debt;
Healed my sickness, gave me sight,
Filled my heart with pure delight!

4 Jesus promised to defend,
    And to be my constant friend:
"Though thy foes be great," said he,
"I will aid and succor thee."

5 In myself, I am unclean.
    Vile and sinful, base and mean;
But in Jesus, I appear
White and comely, bright and fair.

6 In myself, I own it true,
I'm condemned, and justly, too;
But in Jesus, I am free
From the law that threatens me.

7 In myself, I'm led to see
I am worse than poverty;
But in Jesus I possess
Riches, fame, and righteousness.

8 In myself I soon must die;
In the dust my flesh shall lie;
But in Jesus, (wondrous thought!)
I shall live his days throughout!

9 'Tis enough! I ask no more:
Jesus hath laid up in store,
Riches, honor, life and peace—
Joys divine, that never cease!

10 Stranger! wilt thou go with me?
Christ hath plenteous grace for thee:
Wilt thou leave thy carnal toys,
For the Lord's eternal joys?

194   P. M.   *Anonymous.*
Conversion.

THERE is a spot, to me more dear,
  Than native vale or mountain;
A spot, from which affection's tear,
  Springs grateful from its fountain.
'Tis not where kindred souls are bound,
  Though this resembles heaven;

    But where I first my Savior found,
      And felt my sins forgiven.

2 Hard was my lot to reach the shore—
    Long tossed upon the ocean;
  Above me was the thunder's roar—
    Beneath, the wave's commotion.
  Darkly the pall of night was thrown
    Around me—faint with terror!
  In that dark hour how did I groan
    And weep for years of error!

3 Sinking and panting, as for breath,
    I knew not help was near me:
  I cried "Oh! save me Lord, from death!
    "Immortal Jesus, hear me!"
  As quick as thought I felt him mine:
    My Savior stood before me!
  I saw his brightness round me shine,
    And shouted "Glory, glory!"

4 O! sacred place! Oh! hallowed spot!
    Where love divine first found me!
  Wherever falls my distant lot,
    My heart shall linger round thee.
  And when from earth I rise, to soar
    Up to my home in heaven;
  Down, will I cast my eyes, once more,
    Where I was first forgiven!

195   C. M.   *Newto*
A Sight of the Cross.

IN evil long I took delight,
    Unawed by shame or fear,

Till a new object struck my sight,
  And stopped my wild career.

I saw one hanging on a tree,
  In agonies and blood;
Who fixed his languid eyes on me,
  As near the cross I stood.

Sure never till my latest breath
  Can I forget that look:
It seemed to charge me with his death,
  Though not a word he spoke.

My conscience felt and owned the guilt,
  And plunged me in despair;
I saw my sins his blood had spilt
  And helped to nail him there.

Alas! I knew not what I did,
  But knew my tears were vain;
Where shall my trembling soul be hid,
  For I the Lord have slain!

A second look he gave, which said,
  "I freely all forgive;
This blood is for thy ransom paid;
  I die that thou mayst live."

With pleasing grief and mournful joy
  My spirit now is filled.
That I should such a life destroy,
  Yet live by him I killed.

196   7s, 6s.   *New*
The Good Physician.

HOW lost was my condition
  Till Jesus made me whole!
There is but one Physician
  Can cure a sin-sick soul!
Next door to death he found me,
  And snatched me from the grave,
To tell to all around me
  His wondrous power to save.

2 The worst of all diseases
  Is light compared with sin;
On every part it seizes,
  But rages most within:
'Tis palsy, plague, and fever,
  And madness, all combined;
And none but a believer
  The least relief can find.

3 From men, great skill professing,
  I thought a cure to gain;
But this proved more distressing,
  And added to my pain:
Some said that nothing ailed me,
  Some gave me up for lost:
Thus every refuge failed me
  And all my hopes were crossed.

4 At length this great Physician
  (How matchless is his grace!)

Accepted my petition,
  And undertook my case:
First gave me sight to view him,
  (For sin my eyes had sealed,)
Then bade me look unto him:
  I looked, and I was healed.

INVITATIONS AND PROMISES.

197   C. M.   *Medley.*

Whosoever will, let him come.—Rev. xxii. 17.

OH, what amazing words of grace
  Are in the gospel found!
Suited to every sinner's case
  Who knows the joyful sound.

2 Poor, sinful, thirsty, fainting souls
  Are freely welcome here;
Salvation like a river rolls,
  Abundant, free, and clear.

3 Come, then, with all your wants and wounds,
  Your every burden bring;
Here love, unchanging love, abounds,
  A deep celestial spring!

4 Whoever will (oh, gracious word!)
  Shall of this stream partake;
Come, thirsty souls, and bless the Lord,
  And drink for Jesus' sake!

5 Millions of sinners, vile as you
    Have here found life and peace ;
Come, then, and prove its virtues too,
    And drink, adore, and bless.

198.   C. M.   *Watts.*
The Faithfulness of God and his Promises.

BEGIN, my tongue, some heavenly theme
    And speak some boundless thing,
The mighty works, or mightier name,
    Of our eternal King.

2 Tell of his wondrous faithfulness,
    And sound his power abroad,
Sing the sweet promise of his grace,
    And the performing God.

3 Proclaim "salvation from the Lord,
    For wretched, dying men ;"
His hand has writ the sacred word
    With an immortal pen.

4 Engraved, as in eternal brass,
    The mighty promise shines ;
Nor can the powers of darkness rase
    Those everlasting lines.

5 [He that can dash whole worlds to death,
    And make them when he please,
He speaks, and that almighty breath
    Fulfills his great decrees.

6 His very word of grace is strong
   As that which built the skies;
The voice that rolls the stars along
   Speaks all the promises.]

199   C. M.   *Dobell.*
The Penitent Invited.

YE burdened souls to Jesus come,
   You need not be afraid;
He loves to hear poor sinners cry,
   He loves to hear them plead.

2 Ye humble souls, to Jesus come,
   'Tis he who made you see
Your wretched, ruined, helpless state—
   Your guilt and misery.

3 Christ is a friend to mourning souls,
   Then why should you despair,
Since Saul and Mary Magdalene
   Found grace and mercy here?

200   L. M.   *Vanmeter.*
The Awakened Sinner.

AWAKENED soul, to Jesus fly,
   He hath a balm to heal thy wound;
Approach his throne, he'll not deny;
   'Tis there, alone, that pardon's found.

2 " I am too guilty to presume
   To call upon his holy name;

I fear his anger would consume
  A wretch so vile and full of shame.

3 Although thy sins as scarlet be,
  His blood can wash those sins away;
His promise is to such as thee,
  Then come, he will not say thee nay.

4 " How can a wretch, so vile as I,
  Expect his mercy to receive;
I fear I shall a sinner die;
  Lord, help a sinner to believe!"

5 The vilest have his mercy found,
  And shared the richest of his store;
He never on a beggar frowned,
  Then trust his grace, and doubt no more.

201 L. M. *Anon.*
The Penitent Suppliant.

BEHOLD a sinner, dearest Lord,
  Encouraged by thy gracious word,
Would venture near to seek that bread
By which thy children here are fed.

2 Do not the humble suit deny,
Of such a guilty wretch as I:
But let me feed on crumbs, though small,
Which from thy children's table fall.

3 I am a sinner, Lord, I own:
By sin and guilt I am undone;
Yet I would wait, and plead and pray,
Since none are empty sent away.

202   L. M.   *Vanmeter.*

A Soul in Distress.

DISTRESSED soul, to Jesus go,
He hath a balm for all thy wo,
Mercy and grace he hath to give;
He bids the dying sinner live.

2 With all thy guilt, and sin, and shame,
Approach the all-atoning Lamb;
Thou shalt his pardoning grace receive;
He bids the guilty sinner live.

3 He asks no price for all his grace,
His merit, blood or righteousness;
Thy heart is all he will receive,
Then, come, poor sinner, come and live.

4 Though guilt and sin like mountains rise,
And seem to reach the upper skies;
Mountains shall move if thou believe;
Rise, laden sinner, rise and live.

203   S. M.   *Newton.*

The Penitent at the Door of Mercy.

HUNGRY, and faint, and poor,
  Behold us, Lord, again,
Assembled at thy Mercy's door,
  Thy bounty to obtain.

2 Thy word invites us nigh,
  Or we must starve indeed;

For we no money have to buy
  No righteousness to plead.

3 The food our spirits want
    Thy hand alone can give:
  O, hear the prayer of faith, and grant
    That we may eat and live.

204   L. M.   *Vanmeter.*
The Heavy Laden Sinner.

LADEN with sin and guilt am I,
  A sinner justly doomed to die;
Had I a thousand worlds to give
They all should go that I might live!

2 Great God! shall I at last lie down,
  Beneath thy wrath, beneath thy frown?
  It were but justice, should I be
  Cut off from happiness and thee.

3 Oh! that I were some harmless bird,
  That can not sin against the Lord!
  Nor be the object of his wrath,
  Nor fear his judgment after death!

4 Were I some beast upon the plain,
  Without a soul to suffer pain!
  A spreading tree, an opening flower,
  That I might never dread his power!

5 The pine can spread, the flower can bloom;
　The bird can sing, the beast can roam;
　But wo! is me, for I must go
　Down to the realms of endless wo!

6 O, Savior! hear a sinner cry,
　And save a wretch condemned to die!
　Thine arm, alone, can reach my case;
　O! magnify thy sovereign grace!

205　　　　　7s.　　　　　*Kent.*
The Wells of Salvation.—Isa. xii. 3.

WATER from salvation's wells,
　　Thirsty sinner, come and draw;
Grace in Jesus' fullness dwells,
　　More than men or angels know.

2 Love's the fountain whence it rose,
　　Who its height or depth can tell?
　Christ the channel whence it flows,
　　O'er the banks of sin to swell.

3 Thousands now around the throne
　　Water from this fountain drew,
　Felt their griefs and sorrows gone,
　　Sung his praise, and so should you.

4 Bring your empty vessels nigh,
　　Cups or flagons, great or small,

To the brim in rich supply,
  Love eternal fills them all.

5 Bring no money, price, or aught,
   Deeds or alms, or pleasing frame,
  Mercy never can be bought—
   Grace is free in Christ the Lamb.

206   C. M.   *Vanmeter.*
"*Come unto me all ye that Labor.*"—Matth. xi. 28.

"COME unto me," the Savior calls,
  "All ye that labor, come;
I'll give you rest from all your toils,
  And will conduct you home.

2 "Come, take my yoke, and learn of me,
   I'm of a lowly mind;
  Ye shall find rest, and I will be
   A covert from the wind.

3 "My yoke is easy, and I'll make
   My burden to be light;
  Then follow me, and for my sake,
   Keep all your garments white.

4 "He that would my disciple be,
   Must daily bear his cross,
  Deny himself and follow me,
   And count the world but dross."

207   S. M.   *Newton.*

The Pool of Bethesda.—John v. 2, 9.

BESIDE the gospel pool,
   Appointed for the poor,
From year to year my helpless soul
   Has waited for a cure.

2 How often have I seen
   The healing waters move,
And others round me, stepping in,
   Their efficacy prove!

3 [But my complaints remain;
   I feel the very same—
As full of guilt, and fear, and pain—
   As when at first I came.

4 Oh, would the Lord appear,
   My malady to heal!
He knows how long I've languished here,
   And what distress I feel.]

5 How often have I thought,
   Why should I longer lie?
Surely the mercy I have sought
   Is not for such as I!

6 But whither can I go?
   There is no other pool
Where streams of sovereign virtue flow
   To make a sinner whole.

7 Here, then, from day to day,
  I'll wait, and hope, and try:
Can Jesus hear a sinner pray,
Yet suffer him to die?

8 No: he is full of grace;
  He never will permit
A soul, that fain would see his face,
  To perish at his feet.

208　　　　　L. M.　　　　　*Watts.*
A Penitent Pleading for Pardon.—Ps. li.

SHOW pity, Lord! O, Lord, forgive;
  Let a repenting rebel live;
Are not thy mercies large and free?
May not a sinner trust in thee?

2 My crimes are great, but not surpass
The power and glory of thy grace;
Great God, thy nature hath no bound,
So let thy pardoning love be found.

3 Oh, wash my soul from every sin,
And make my guilty conscience clean;
Here on my heart the burden lies,
And past offences pain my eyes.

4 My lips with shame my sins confess
Against thy law, against thy grace;
Lord, should thy judgment grow severe,
I am condemned, but thou art clear.

5 Should sudden vengeance seize my breath,
   I must pronounce thee just in death;
   And if my soul were sent to hell,
   Thy righteous law approves it well.

6 Yet save a trembling sinner, Lord,
   Whose hope, still hovering round thy word,
   Would light on some sweet promise there,
   Some sure support against despair.

THE CHRISTIAN.

209   C. M.   *Watts.*

Holy Fortitude.—1 Cor. xvi. 13.

AM I a soldier of the cross,
   A follower of the Lamb?
And shall I fear to own his cause,
   Or blush to speak his name?

2 Must I be carried to the skies
   On flowery beds of ease;
While others fought to win the prize,
   And sailed through bloody seas?

3 Are there no foes for me to face?
   Must I not stem the flood?
Is this vile world a friend to grace,
   To help me on to God?

4 Sure I must fight, if I would reign :
　　Increase my courage, Lord !
I'll bear the toil, endure the pain,
　　Supported by thy word.

5 Thy saints in all this glorious war
　　Shall conquer though they die ;
They see the triumph from afar,
　　And seize it with their eye.

6 When that illustrious day shall rise,
　　And all thine armies shine
In robes of victory through the skies,
　　The glory shall be thine.

210　　　　　8s.　　　　*Parkinso.*

Experience.

I AM a stranger here below,
　　And what I am is hard to know ;
I am so vile, so prone to sin,
I fear that I'm not born again.

2 Would I experience call to mind,—
I often find myself so blind,
All marks of grace seem to be gone,
Which makes me fear that I am wrong.

3 I find myself out of the way ;
My thoughts are often gone astray ;

Like one alone I seem to be :
Oh, is there any one like me ?

4 'Tis seldom I can ever see
Myself as I would wish to be ;
What I desire I can't retain,
From what I hate I can't refrain.

5 So far from God I seem to lie,
That often I'm constrained to cry ;
I fear at last that I shall fall,
Or, if a saint, I'm least of all.

6 I seldom find a heart to pray,
So many things come in the way ;
Thus filled with doubts, I ask to know,
Come tell me if 'tis thus with you ?

7 By sore experience I do know
There's nothing good that I can do ;
I cannot satisfy the law,
Nor hope nor comfort from it draw.

3 My nature is so prone to sin,
And all my duties so unclean,
That, when I count up all the cost,
Without free grace I know I'm lost.

211 L. M. *Vanmeter.*
The Christian Warfare.—Rom. vii.

FULL of vain thoughts and worldly cares,
Oft I am made, with Paul, to cry,

'Midst my temptations, doubts and fears:
"Oh! what a wretched man am I!"

2 Though oft the throne I supplicate,
That I may from such evils fly;
Yet do the very things I hate:
"Oh! what a wretched man am I!"

3 Sold under sin, I always find
My flesh opposed to the most High;
Not to his sovereign will resigned:
"Oh! What a wretched man am I!"

4 The law is holy, just and good,
But I cannot with it comply;
I cannot do the things I would:
"Oh! what a wretched man am I!"

5 'Tis thus the Spirit and the flesh,
Both strive to gain the victory;
Each day I feel the war afresh:
"Oh! what a wretched man am I!"

6 But hark! I hear my Savior's voice!
My soul shall on his grace rely;
He bids me in his name rejoice,
For he hath gained the victory.

212   L. M.   *Parkinson's*
Self-Examination.

WHAT strange perplexities arise!
What anxious fears and jealousies!

What crowds in doubtful light appear!
How few, alas! approved and clear!

And what am I? My soul, awake,
And an impartial survey take;
Does no dark sign, no ground of fear,
In practice or in heart appear?

What image does my spirit bear?
Is Jesus formed and living there?
Say, do his lineaments divine
In thought, and word, and action shine?

Searcher of hearts, oh, search me still;
The secrets of my soul reveal;
My fears remove. Let me appear
To God and my own conscience clear.

3   S. M.   *Newton.*
Lamentations i. 14.

LORD, can a soul like mine,
   Unholy and unclean,
Dare venture near a throne of grace,
   With such a load of sin?

If I attempt to pray,
   And lisp thy holy name,
My thoughts are hurried soon away;
   I know not where I am.

If in thy word I look,
   Such darkness fills my mind,

I only read a sealed book,
　　　　But no relief can find.

4　Myself can hardly bear
　　　This wretched heart of mine;
　How hateful then must it appear
　　　To those pure eyes of thine!

5　That blood which Jesus spilt,
　　　That grace which is thine own,
　Can cleanse the vilest sinner's guilt,
　　　And soften hearts of stone.

6　Low at thy feet I bow,
　　　Oh, pity and forgive!
　Here will I lie and wait till thou
　　　Shalt bid me rise and live.

214　　　　L. M.　　　　*Vanmeter.*
　　Gratitude for Past Blessings.

AND yet, the Lord remembers me!
　　　He still protects me by his power;
Each day his bounteous hand I see;
　　His grace upholds me every hour.

2　Though oft I do forgetful prove,
　　　His love to me is still the same;
　And yet, for such unchanging love,
　　　My thanks and my returns how lame!

3　Through many dangers I have come,
　　　Where death appeared on every hand;

Others have sunk into the tomb,
  While I through grace, am left to stand!

I'll sing the goodness of the Lord,
  While he permits me here to stay;
And after death I will record,
  His grace throughout an endless day.

115   8s and 7s.   *Robinson.*
  Ebenezer.—1 Sam. vii. 12.

COME, thou Fount of every blessing,
  Tune my heart to sing thy grace:
Streams of mercy, never ceasing,
  Call for songs of loudest praise:
Teach me some melodious sonnet,
  Sung by flaming tongues above;
Praise the mount! Oh, fix me on it,—
  Mount of thy redeeming love.

Here I raise my Ebenezer,
  Hither by thy help I'm come;
And I trust by thy good pleasure,
  Safely to arrive at home.
Jesus sought me when a stranger,
  Wandering from the fold of God;
He to rescue me from danger,
  Interposed his precious blood!

Oh, to grace how great a debtor
  Daily I'm constrained to be!
Let thy grace, Lord, like a fetter,
  Bind my wandering heart to thee;

Prone to wander, Lord, I feel it;
　Prone to leave the God I love;
Here's my heart: oh, take and seal it!
　Seal it for thy courts above.

216　　　　　C. M.　　　　　*Vanmeter.*
Hope, the Anchor of the Soul.

THOUGH sin and Satan both unite,
　To overcome my hope;
Jesus, in whom is my delight,
　I trust will bear me up.

2 Why should I dread the storms that rise,
　And howl around my head;
Since Jesus manages the skies,
　And promises his aid?

3 Though tempests blow and billows roll,
　And though my bark is frail;
Yet hope, the anchor of my soul,
　Is cast within the vail.

4 Why should I shun to bear my cross,
　And undergo the shame;
Since earth's best treasures are but dross,
　Compared with Jesus' name?

5 Why should I dread cold Jordan's wave?
　'Tis but a narrow stream?
Why need I shudder at the grave,
　Since Jesus can redeem?

6 Yes, when the earth, and time, shall end,
    Jesus, in whom I trust,
  Will come, and like a faithful Friend,
    Reanimate my dust.

217　　　　L. M.　　　　*Beddome.*
Patience.

DEAR Lord, though bitter is the cup
    Thy gracious hand deals out to me,
  I cheerfully will drink it up:
    That cannot hurt which comes from thee.

2 'Tis full of thine unchanging love,
    Nor can a drop of wrath be there;
  The saints forever blest above
    Were often most afflicted here.

3 From Jesus, thy incarnate Son,
    I'll learn obedience to thy will,
  And humbly kiss the chastening rod
    When its severest strokes I feel.

218　　　　C. M.　　　　*Vanmeter.*
"My Leanness, My Leanness."—Isa. 24, 16.

HOW cold and barren is my soul!
    How lifeless is my heart!
  While doubts and troubles o'er me roll,
    And gloomy hours impart.

2 There was a time I thought I loved
    The Savior's precious name;

But how have my affections roved
   And brought my soul to shame?

3 Where is the joy? where is the peace,
   That made my heart so glad?
 If I e'er tasted of his grace,
   Why, now, am I so sad?

4 How often am I led to fear,
   That I have been deceived;
 So few the marks of grace appear,
   I fear I've not believed.

5 Dear Savior! if I'm thine, indeed,
   Reclaim this wandering heart!
 If not, Oh! cause it, Lord, to bleed!
   Eternal life impart.

219   8, 8, 6.   *R. Hill.*
         1 Timothy 6, 8.

TELL me no more of earthly toys,
   Of sinful mirth and carnal joys,
   The things I loved before;
 Let me but view my Savior's face,
 And feel his animating grace,
   And I desire no more.

2 Tell me no more of praise and wealth,
 Tell me no more of ease and health,
   For these have all their snares;

Let me but know my sins forgiven,
And see my name enrolled in heaven,
 And I am free from cares.

3 Tell me no more of lofty towers,
Delightful gardens, fragrant bowers,
 For these are trifling things;
The little room for me designed,
Will suit as well my easy mind,
 As palaces of kings.

4 Tell me no more of crowded guests,
Of sumptuous feasts and gaudy dress,
 Extravagance and waste;
My little table only spread
With wholesome herbs and wholesome bread,
 Will better suit my taste.

5 Give me the bible in my hand,
A heart to read and understand,
 And faith to trust the Lord:
I'd sit alone from day to day,
Nor urge my company to stay,
 Nor wish to rove abroad.

220   L. M.   *Watts.*
John i. 12.

NOT all the nobles of the earth,
 Who boast the honors of their birth,
Such real dignity can claim
As those who bear the Christian name.

2 To them the privilege is given
 To be the sons and heirs of heaven;
 Sons of the God who reigns on high,
 And heirs of joy beyond the sky.

3 On them, a happy chosen race,
 Their Father pours his richest grace;
 To them his counsels he imparts,
 And stamps his image on their hearts.

4 When, through temptation, they rebel,
 His chastening rod he makes them feel;
 Then, with a father's tender heart,
 He soothes the pain, and heals the smart.

221   L. M.   *Vanmeter.*

The Christian, Calm in Life and in Death.

THE child of God, how highly blessed,
 Of honors, life and peace possessed;
How calm his life, serene his path,
When he can walk the road by faith.

2 Though storm and tempest round him rise,
 Calmly he views the troubled skies;
 And knows that God, the God of grace,
 Can bid the storm and tempest cease.

3 Though persecution wield the sword,
 His faith is centered in the Lord;
 Nor death, nor hell shall him affright,
 For still he trusts the God of might.

4 And when his final hour appears,
   Jesus will calm his rising fears,
   And bid his parting voice to sing
   A triumph o'er the monster's sting.

222   C. M.   *Newton.*
             Amazing Grace.

AMAZING grace! (how sweet the sound!)
   That saved a wretch like me;
I once was lost, but now am found;
   Was blind, but now I see.

2 'Twas grace that taught my heart to fear,
   And grace my fears relieved;
How precious did that grace appear
   The hour I first believed!

3 Through many dangers, toils, and snares,
   I have already come;
'Tis grace has brought me safe thus far,
   And grace will lead me home.

4 The Lord has promised good to me;
   His word my hope secures;
He will my shield and portion be,
   As long as life endures.

5 Yes, when this flesh and heart shall fail,
   And mortal life shall cease,
I shall possess within the veil
   A life of joy and peace.

6 The earth shall soon dissolve like snow,
    The sun forbear to shine,
But God, who called me here below,
    Will be forever mine.

223   C. M.   *Vanmeter.*
Joy over Conversion.

O HOW melodious was that voice,
    Which bade my sins depart!
That filled my soul with heavenly joys,
    And healed my broken heart!

2 'Twas Jesus spake: and at his word,
    My load of guilt was gone!
I leaped for joy, and praised the Lord,
    For what his grace had done!

3 My soul was bordering on despair,
    And sinking down with grief;
When Jesus, Savior, saw me there,
    And ran to my relief.

4 O! wondrous love! that snatched my feet,
    From the abyss of wo!
Here, all my warmest passions meet.
    And hence my comforts flow.

224   7s.   *Newton.*
Lovest Thou Me?—John xxi. 16.

'TIS a point I long to know,
    Oft it causes anxious thought:—

Do I love the Lord, or no?
　　Am I his or am I not?

2 If I love, why am I thus?
　　Why this dull and lifeless frame?
　Hardly, sure, can they be worse
　　Who have never heard his name.

3 [Could my heart so hard remain,
　　Prayer a task and burden prove,
　Every trifle give me pain,
　　If I knew a Savior's love?

4 When I turn my eyes within,
　　All is dark, and vain, and wild,
　Filled with unbelief and sin,
　　Can I deem myself a child?]

5 If I pray, or hear, or read,
　　Sin is mixed with all I do:
　You that love the Lord indeed,
　　Tell me, is it thus with you?

6 Yet I mourn my stubborn will,
　　Find my sin a grief and thrall;
　Should I grieve for what I feel,
　　If I did not love at all?

7 [Could I joy his saints to meet,
　　Choose the ways I once abhorred,
　Find at times the promise sweet
　　If I did not love the Lord?]

8 Lord, decide the doubtful case;
  Thou, who art thy people's Sun,
Shine upon thy work of grace,
  If it be indeed begun.

9 Let me love thee more and more,
  If I love at all, I pray!
If I have not loved before,
  Help me to begin to-day.

225 . L. M. *Van*

Christian Enquiry.

HOW can I be a child of grace,
  While my affections are so cold?
How could my heart remain so base,
  If I belonged to Jesus' fold?

2 When I enjoy prosperity,
  My sinful heart grows proud and vain;
And when I feel adversity,
  How apt to murmur and complain.

3 When I behold the crooked path
  In which my roving feet have trod,
And feel the weakness of my faith,
  How can I be a child of God?

4 When I approach before his throne,
  To lay my griefs and sorrows there;
How oft I find my heart is prone,
  To rove and wander off elsewhere?

5 Through doubts and darkness oft I go,
　　And seem to reach the shades of death :
　Ye saints of God, I ask to know,
　　Have you e'er traveled in this path ?

6 I want to serve the Lord, I know,
　　But such is my imperfect state,
　The things I would I cannot do,
　　Yet do the very things I hate.

7 Oh! gracious Lord, decide my case !
　　Increase my faith, if I am thine :
　If not, oh ! cause thy sovereign grace
　　In my benighted soul to shine !

226　　　　L. M.　　　　*Fawcett.*

Remembering all the way the Lord has led him.—
　　　　Deut. viii. 2.

THUS far my God hath led me on,
　And made his truth and mercy known,
My hopes and fears alternate rise,
And comforts mingle with my sighs.

2 Through this wide wilderness I roam,
　Far distant from my blissful home ;
　Lord, let thy presence be my stay,
　And guard me in this dangerous way.

3 Temptations everywhere annoy,
　And sins and snares my peace destroy :
　My earthly joys are from me torn,
　And oft an absent God I mourn.

4 My soul with various tempests tossed,
   Her hopes o'erturned, her projects crossed,
   Sees every day new straits attend,
   And wonders where the scene will end.

5 Is this, dear Lord, that thorny road
   Which leads us to the mount of God?
   Are these the toils thy people know
   While in the wilderness below?

6 'Tis even so: thy faithful love
   Doth all thy children's graces prove;
   'Tis thus our pride and self must fall,
   That Jesus may be All in All.

227   L. M.   *Vanmeter.*
Reflections at the End of the Year.

WHEN all thy mercies I survey,
   Or try to count thy blessings o'er,
Lord, they are like a boundless sea,
   Or like the sand upon the shore!

2 Through all the dangers of the year,
   Thy hand, unseen, hath led me on;
By night and day thy guardian care
   Hath been to me, a sinner, shown.

3 Death hath its thousands round me slain;
   Affliction seized its thousands more;
And yet my life and health remain:
   O! Lord, I would thy name adore!

4 My daily wants have been supplied,
    While some have begged their scanty bread!
Thy bounteous hand hath not denied,
    My humble board with food to spread!

5 But ah! ingratitude of heart!
    How oft have I my friend forgot!
Been ready from him to depart,
    And yet his kindness changes not!

6 What poor returns of love I pay
    To him for blessings so divine!
Lord! may I give myself away,
    For I, and all I have, are thine.

228   C. M.   *Cowper.*
Walking with God.—Gen. v. 24.

OH for a closer walk with God,
    A calm and heavenly frame,
A light to shine upon the road
    That leads me to the Lamb!

2 Where is the blessedness I knew
    When first I saw the Lord?
Where is the soul-refreshing view
    Of Jesus and his word?

3 What peaceful hours I then enjoyed!
    How sweet their memory still!
But now I find an aching void
    The world can never fill.

4 Return, O Holy Dove! return,
　　Sweet messenger of rest!
　I hate the sins that made thee mourn
　　And drove thee from my breast.

5 The dearest idol I have known,
　　Whate'er that idol be,
　Help me to tear it from thy throne,
　　And worship only thee.

6 So shall my walk be close with God,
　　Calm and serene my frame;
　So purer light shall mark the road
　　That leads me to the Lamb.

229　　　　　　L. M.　　　　　*Vanmeter.*
The Carnal and the Spiritual Mind.—Rom. viii. 6.

WHAT little comfort do we find,
　When we indulge a carnal mind?
But when the spirit rules the heart,
What life and peace it doth impart!

2 When we allow the world to rise
　In estimation in our eyes;
　It kills our life, and peace, and joy,
　And our religious comforts die.

3 But when the heavenly mind prevails
　The earth, with all its pleasure, fails
　To show an object of delight,
　But shrinks to nothing in our sight.

4 Betwixt the new man and the old,
  A constant warfare we behold;
  But grace shall yet a conqueror be,
  And wear a crown of victory.

5 The younger shall have his desire:
  The love of God, that holy fire,
  Shall reign, and rule, and mount on high,
  Till flesh and blood grow old and die.

230   7s.   *Swain.*

Mutual Encouragement.

BRETHREN, while we sojourn here,
  Fight we must, but should not fear;
Foes we have, but we've a Friend,
One that loves us to the end.
Forward, then, with courage go,
Long we shall not dwell below;
Soon the joyful news will come,
"Child, your Father calls: Come home."

2 In the way a thousand snares
  Lie, to take us unawares;
  Satan, with malicious art,
  Watches each unguarded part:
  But from Satan's malice free
  Saints shall soon victorious be;
  Soon the joyful news will come,
  "Child, your Father calls: Come home."

3 But, of all the foes we meet,
  None so oft mislead our feet,

None betray us into sin,
Like the foes that dwell within.
Yet let nothing spoil your peace,
Christ will also conquer these;
Then the joyful news will come,
"Child, your Father calls: Come home."

231   8s.   *Newton.*

None Upon the Earth I Desire but Thee.—Ps. lxxiii. 24.

HOW tedious and tasteless the hours
   When Jesus no longer I see!
Sweet prospects, sweet birds, and sweet flowers
   Have all lost their sweetness to me:
The midsummer sun shines but dim,
   The fields strive in vain to look gay;
But when I am happy in him,
   December's as pleasant as May.

2 His name yields the richest perfume,
   And sweeter than music his voice;
His presence disperses my gloom,
   And makes all within me rejoice:
I should, were he always thus nigh,
   Have nothing to wish or to fear;
No mortal so happy as I,
   My summer would last all the year.

3 Content with beholding his face,
   My all to his pleasure resigned,
No changes of season or place
   Would make any change in my mind:

While blessed with a sense of his love,
  A palace a toy would appear,
And prisons would palaces prove
  If Jesus would dwell with me there.

4 Dear Lord, if indeed I am thine,
  If thou art my sun and my song,
Say, why do I languish and pine,
  And why are my winters so long?
Oh, drive these dark clouds from my sky,
  Thy soul-cheering presence restore;
Or take me unto thee on high,
  Where winter and clouds are no more.

232   7s. & 6s.   *Vanmeter.*

"*My Times are in thy Hand.*"—Ps. xxxi. 15.

COME, all ye humble pilgrims,
  And listen to my song;
And I will try to tell you
  How I do get along:
I pass through many changes
  On the celestial road;
Sometimes I'm doubting whether
  I'm on the way to God.

2 Sometimes I'm carnal minded,
  And all my comforts cease;
Sometimes I'm in the Spirit,
  And then I've joy and peace,
Sometimes, by faith, I triumph,
  O'er Satan and his band,
Sometimes I meet temptations
  That I cannot withstand.

3 Sometimes I'm cold and stupid,
    And duty seems a load;
Sometimes it is a pleasure
    To praise and worship God.
Sometimes, upon the willows
    My mournful harp is hung;
Sometimes I find my Savior,
    And then my harp is strung.

4 Sometimes I walk in darkness,
    With scarce a ray of light;
Sometimes the sun arises,
    And breaks the shades of night.
Sometimes the Holy Bible
    My condemnation reads;
Sometimes I find a treasure
    Of grace for all my needs.

5 Sometimes I am much troubled,
    For fear I've been deceived;
Sometimes my Savior whispers:
    "You have on me believed."
Sometimes I hear the gospel,
    And on its dainties feast;
Sometimes I have no relish,
    And do not get a taste.

6 Sometimes I think of dying,
    And fear that dreadful day;
Sometimes by faith I'm flying,
    And long to soar away:

Oh! when shall I leave trials,
And be conducted home!
Where there shall be no changes,
And troubles never come!

233 11s. K——

Exceeding Great and Precious Promises.—1 Pet. i. 4.

HOW firm a foundation, ye saints of the Lord,
Is laid for your faith in his excellent word!
What more can he say than to you he hath said?
You, who unto Jesus for refuge have fled.

2 In every condition, in sickness, in health,
In poverty's vale, or abounding in wealth,
At home and abroad, on the land, on the sea,
As thy days may demand, shall thy strength ever be.

3 Fear not: I am with thee; oh, be not dismayed!
I, I am thy God, and will still give thee aid;
I'll strengthen thee, help thee, and cause thee to stand,
Upheld by my righteous, omnipotent hand.

4 When through the deep waters I call thee to go,
The rivers of wo shall not thee overflow;
For I will be with thee, thy troubles to bless,
And sanctify to thee thy deepest distress.

5 When through fiery trials thy pathway shall lie,
My grace, all-sufficient, shall be thy supply;
The flame shall not hurt thee: I only design
Thy dross to consume, and thy gold to refine.

6 Even down to old age, all my people shall prove
My sovereign, eternal, unchangeable love;
And, when hoary hairs shall their temples adorn,
Like lambs they shall still in my bosom be borne.

7 The soul that on Jesus hath leaned for repose
I will not, I will not desert to his foes;
That soul, though all hell should endeavor to shake,
I'll never, no, *never*, no, *never forsake*.

234   P. M.   *Dupuy's Selec.*

WHAT wondrous love is this, O my soul, O my soul,
What wondrous love is this, O my soul?
What wondrous love is this, that caused the Lord of bliss
To bear the dreadful curse for my soul, for my soul,
To bear the dreadful curse for my soul?

2 When I was sinking down, sinking down, sinking down,
When I was sinking down, sinking down,
When I was sinking down beneath God's righteous frown,
Christ laid aside his crown for my soul, for my soul,
Christ laid aside his crown for my soul.

3 Ye winged seraphs, fly, bear the news, bear the news,
Ye winged seraphs, fly, bear the news,

Ye winged seraphs, fly, like comets through the sky,
Fill vast eternity with the news, with the news;
Fill vast eternity with the news.

4 To God and to the Lamb I will sing, I will sing,
To God and to the Lamb I will sing,
To God and to the Lamb, and to the great I AM,
While millions join the theme, I will sing, I will sing,
While millions join the theme I will sing.

5 Ye sons of Zion's King, join the praise, join the praise,
Ye sons of Zion's King, join the praise,
Ye sons of Zion's King, with hearts and voices sing,
And strike each tuneful string in his praise, in his praise,
And strike each tuneful string in his praise.

235 S. M. *Vanmeter.*
God's Love in Adoption.—1 John iii, 1.

BEHOLD! what wondrous love
  The Father hath bestowed
Upon us sinners, that we should
  Be called the sons of God!

2 It doth not yet appear,
  How great the saints shall be;
But when the archangel's trump we hear,
  We shall our Savior see.

3 Then shall we all awake,
 And in his likeness shine:
Be satisfied when we partake
 Of glories so divine!

4 These bodies that are sown
 In weakness, he shall raise
In power, and fashion like his own,
 And we shall sing his praise.

5 Enough, my soul replies!
 His goodness I'll adore!
Since I shall in his likeness rise,
 I can desire no more!

236   8s. & 7s.   *Christian Psalmist.*

DARK and thorny is the desert
 Through which pilgrims make their way;
But beyond this vale of sorrow
 Lie the realms of endless day.
Dear young soldiers, do not murmur
 At the troubles of the way;
Meet the tempest, fight with courage,
 Never faint, but often pray.

2 He whose thunder shakes creation;
 He that bids the planets roll;
He that rides upon the tempest,
 And whose scepter sways the whole;
Jesus, Jesus, will defend you;
 Trust in him, and him alone;
He has shed his blood to save you,
 And will bring you to his throne,

3 There on flowery fields of pleasure
   And the hills of endless rest,
  Joy, and peace, and love, shall ever
   Reign and triumph in our breast.
  There ten thousand flaming seraphs
   Fly across the heavenly plain;
  There they sing immortal praises!
   Glory, glory is their theme.

4 But, methinks, a sweeter concert
   Makes the crystal arches ring,
  And a song is heard in Zion
   Which the angels cannot sing;
  Who can paint those sons of glory,
   Ransomed souls that dwell on high,
  Who with golden harps for ever
   Sound redemption through the sky.

237   L. M.   *Vanmeter*

"*All Things Work Together for Good.*"—
    Romans viii. 28.

WHAT heavenly comfort do we find,
   To cheer the drooping saints of God?
The Book declares, all things combined
   Shall work together for their good.

2 Though they are through the furnace led,
   Or through the storm, or through the flood;
  They call to mind that he hath said:
   "All things" shall prove to be their good.

3 Though persecution draws the sword,
   And drives the church thro' seas of blood;

She trusts her ever faithful Lord,
  Shall over-rule it for her good.

4 Though tribulations may surround,
    And thorns infest her heavenly road;
  They may distress; but will be found
    To work together for her good.

5 Yes, for her sake, all nations stand;
    For her the Savior spilt his blood:
  He hath all things at his command,
    And makes them end in Zion's good.

6 And when her sufferings here shall end,
    And she surrounds the throne of God;
  This heavenly anthem shall ascend:
    "All things have ended in our good."

238   L. M.   *Hoskins.*
            John ix. 25.

NOW let my soul with wonder trace
    The Savior's miracles of grace;
  Now let my lips and life record
  The loving kindness of the Lord.

2 Till late I fancied all was well,
  Though walking in the road to hell;
  But now, through grace divinely free,
  I who was blind, am brought to see.

3 Long had I slept in nature's night,
  But Jesus came and gave me light!
  Ten thousand praises, Lord, to thee,
  That though once blind, yet now I see!

4 Long I had wallowed in my sin,
   Blind to the danger I was in;
   But now appeal, great God, to thee,
   That though once blind, yet now I see!

5 Long did I on the law rely,
   And pass the Friend of sinners by;
   But what a glorious mystery!
   Though I was blind, yet now I see!

6 Strengthen, O Lord, my mental sight;
   Increase my faith, increase my light;
   Then shall I praise the sacred Three,
   In time and in eternity.

239   S. M.   *Watts.*

God all and in all.—Ps. lxxiii. 25.

MY God, my life, my love,
   To thee, to thee, I call,
I cannot live if thou remove,
   For thou art all in all.

2 [Thy shining grace can cheer
   This dungeon where I dwell;
'Tis paradise when thou art here,
   If thou depart, 'tis hell.

3 [Not all the harps above
   Can make a heavenly place,
If God his residence remove,
   Or but conceal his face.]

4 Nor earth, nor all the sky,
　　Can one delight afford,
　No, not a drop of real joy,
　　Without thy presence, Lord.

5 Thou art the sea of love
　　Where all my pleasures roll,
　The circle where my passions move,
　　And center of my soul.

6 [To thee my spirits fly
　　With infinite desire,
　And yet how far from thee I lie!
　　Dear Jesus, raise me nigher.]

240　　　　　S. M.　　　　　*Watts.*

Heavenly Joy on Earth.

COME, we that love the Lord,
　　And let our joys be known;
Join in a song of sweet accord,
　　And thus surround the throne.

2 The sorrows of the mind
　　Be banished from the place!
　Religion never was designed
　　To make our pleasures less.

3 Let those refuse to sing
　　That never knew our God,
　But favorites of the heavenly King
　　May speak their joys abroad.

4 [The God that rules on high,
　　And thunders when he please,
　That rides upon the stormy sky,
　　And manages the seas:

5 This awful God is ours,
　　Our Father and our love;
　He will send down his heavenly powers
　　To carry us above.

6 There we shall see his face,
　　And never, never sin;
　There from the rivers of his grace
　　Drink endless pleasures in.]

241　　　　　C. M.　　　　　*Vanmeter.*

Trust in the Name of Jesus.—Acts iv. 12.

THE name of Jesus is my trust:
　　None other name is given
Among the bright angelic host—
　　None other under heaven.

2 No other name could take the book,
　　And loose the seals thereof:
None other hath our sorrows took.
　　Nor shown us half the love.

3 Eternal life is treasured up
　　In this dear Lamb of God:
On him I build my only hope
　　Nor fear the raging flood.

4 Through all our trials here below,
  Lord, guide our wandering feet;
And when we leave this world of wo,
  May we our Savior meet.

HEAVENLY PROSPECTS.

242   L. M.   *Parkinson's Selec.*
Hopes of Heaven Drown Cares on Earth.—Heb. xiii. 14.

WE'VE no abiding city here:
  This may distress the worldling's mind,
But should not cost the saint a tear,
  Who hopes a better rest to find.

2 "We've no abiding city here;"
  Sad truth, were this to be our home:
But let this thought our spirits cheer:
  "We seek a city yet to come."

3 "We've no abiding city here;"
  Then let us live as pilgrims do;
Let not the world our rest appear,
  But let us haste from all below.

4 "We've no abiding city here;"
  We seek a city out of sight:
Zion its name,—we'll soon be there;
  It shines with everlasting light.

5 Oh, sweet abode of peace and love!
    Where pilgrims freed from toil are blest:
  Had I the pinions of a dove,
    I'd fly to thee and be at rest.

6 But hush, my soul, nor dare repine;
    The time my God appoints is best;
  While here, to do his will be mine,
    And his to fix my time of rest.

243   C. M.   *Stennett.*
          The Promised Land.

ON Jordan's stormy banks I stand,
    And cast a wishful eye
  To Canaan's fair and happy land,
    Where my possessions lie.

2 Oh, the transporting, rapturous scene
    That rises to my sight!
  Sweet fields arrayed in living green,
    And rivers of delight!

3 There generous fruits, that never fail,
    On trees immortal grow;
  There rocks and hills, and brooks and vales,
    With milk and honey flow.

4 All o'er those wide-extended plains
    Shines one eternal day;
  There God the Sun forever reigns,
    And scatters night away.

5 No chilling wind, nor poisonous breath,
   Can reach that healthful shore;
Sickness and sorrow, pain and death,
   Are felt and feared no more.

6 When shall I reach that happy place
   And be forever blest?
When shall I see my Father's face,
   And in his bosom rest?

7 Filled with delight, my raptured soul
   Can here no longer stay;
Though Jordan's waves around me roll,
   Fearless I'll launch away.

244   L. M.   *Watts.*
Longing for Heaven.

I'M bound for New Jerusalem,
   Thither my best-beloved is gone;
The righteous branch of Jesse's stem,
   'Tis he I've fixed my heart upon.

2 [Fain would I climb above the skies,
   To see the beauties of his face;
My faith would into vision rise,
   And hope would cease in his embrace.]

3 I languish with extreme desire
   The object of my love to see;
Oh, let me in love's flames expire,
   That I may with my Jesus be.

4 This life's a pilgrimage of care;
    When will the happy season come,
  That I shall breathe celestial air
    And settle in my native home?

5 I long to reach the shore of bliss,
    And see the New Jerusalem;
  Where my beloved Jesus is.
    And spend eternity with him.

245 C. M. *Eckington's Col.*
The Heavenly Jerusalem.

JERUSALEM, my happy home,
    Oh, how I long for thee!
  When will my sorrows have an end?
    Thy joys when shall I see?

2 Thy walls are all of precious stone,
    Most glorious to behold;
  Thy gates are richly set with pearl,
    Thy streets are paved with gold.

3 Thy garden and thy pleasant green
    My study long have been:
  Such sparkling light by human sight
    Has never yet been seen.

4 If heaven be thus so glorious, Lord,
    Why should I stay from thence?
  What folly 'tis, that I should dread
    To die and go from hence!

5 Jesus, my love, to glory's gone;
   Him will I go and see;
And all my brethren here below
   Will soon come after me.

6 When we've been there ten thousand years,
   Bright-shining as the sun,
We've no less days to sing God's praise
   Than when we first begun.

246   8s.   *Christian Psalmist.*

WE speak of the realms of the blest,
   That country so bright and so fair;
And oft are its glories confessed,
   But what must it be to be there?

2 We speak of its freedom from sin,
   From sorrow, temptation, and care,
From trials without and within—
   But what must it be to be there?

3 We speak of its service of love,
   The robes which the glorified wear,
The church of the first-born above—
   But what must it be to be there?

4 Oh Lord, in this valley of wo,
   Our spirits for heaven prepare,
And shortly we also shall know,
   And feel what it is to be there.

247   10s.   *Vanmeter.*

Heaven.

'TWAS far above the earth I fixed mine eyes,
   And lo! I saw a region 'bove the skies,
Arrayed in peerless light and glory, far
Exceeding sun, and moon, and morning star.

2 A city, grand and lofty, paved with gold;
   Filled with seraphic joys which can't be told:
Salvation's walls encompass it around,
And naught but glorious forms is in it found.

3 There stands the Tree of Life, divinely fair,
   Spreading its boughs in the ambrosial air;
And from its base an ancient river flows,
To water all this region of repose.

4 There sits, enthroned, amid this bright abode,
   A conquering King, the exalted Lamb of God;
Around whose feet, a bright, angelic throng,
And men redeemed, join in an endless song.

5 Refulgent beams through all this region spread
   Eternal day round the Redeemer's head:
He calls his spouse, for whom he bled and died,
To enter in, and seats her by his side.

6 While thus beholding heaven's celestial plains,
   My ears saluted with immortal strains,
I longed to leave these earthly shores, and fly,
To realize the glories of the sky!

248 10s. (*Tune, Amboy.*)
A Home in Heaven.

A HOME in heaven! what a joyful thought!
As the poor man toils in his weary lot;
His heart oppressed, and with anguish riven,
From his home below to a home in heaven.

2 A home in heaven! as the sufferer lies
On his bed of pain, and uplifts his eyes
To that bright home, what a joy is given,
With the blessed thought of a home in heaven!

3 A home in heaven! when our pleasures fade,
And our wealth and fame in the dust are laid;
And our strength decays, and our health is riven,
We are happy still with our home in heaven.

4 A home in heaven! when the sinner mourns,
And with contrite heart to the Savior turns;
Oh! then what bliss in that heart forgiven,
Does the hope inspire of a home in heaven.

5 A home in heaven! when our friends are fled,
To the cheerless grave of the mouldering dead;
We wait in hope of the promise given,
We will meet again in our home in heaven.

249 P. M. *Christian Psalmist.*
The Heavenly Clime.

HAVE you heard, have you heard of that heavenly clime,
Undimmed by sorrow, unhurt by time,

HEAVENLY PROSPECTS.

Where age hath no power o'er the fadeless frame,
Where the eye is fire, and the heart is flame—
Have you heard of that heavenly clime?

2 A river of water gushes there,
'Mid flowers of beauty strangely fair,
And a thousand wings are hovering o'er,
The dazzling wave and the golden shore,
That are seen in that heavenly clime.

3 Millions of forms, all clothed in bright,
In garments of beauty, clear and white—
They dwell in their own immortal bowers,
'Mid fadeless hues of countless flowers,
That bloom in that heavenly clime.

4 Ear hath not heard, and eye hath not seen,
Their swelling song and their changeless sheen,
Their ensigns are waving, their banners unfurled
O'er jasper walls and gates of pearl,
That are fixed in that heavenly clime.

5 But far, far away in that sinless clime,
Undimmed by sorrow, unhurt by time;
Where amid all things that's fair is given,
The home of the just—and its name is Heaven,
The name of that sinless clime.

250 C. M. *Watts.*
View of Heaven.

THERE is a land of pure delight,
Where saints immortal reign;

Infinite day excludes the night,
  And pleasures banish pain.

2 There everlasting spring abides,
  And never-withering flowers:
Death like a narrow sea, divides
  This heavenly land from ours.

3 Sweet fields, beyond the swelling flood,
  Stand dressed in living green;
So to the Jews old Canaan stood,
  While Jordan rolled between.

4 But timorous mortals start and shrink
  To cross this narrow sea,
And linger, shivering, on the brink,
  And fear to launch away.

5 Oh! could we make our doubts remove,
  Those gloomy doubts that rise,
And see the Canaan that we love,
  With unbeclouded eyes,—

6 Could we but climb where Moses stood,
  And view the landscape o'er,—
Not Jordan's stream, nor death's cold flood,
  Should fright us from the shore.

251   C. M. *Dover's Selec.*
Death and Heavenly Happiness.

AND let this feeble body fail,
  And let it faint or die!
My soul shall quit this mournful vale,
  And soar to worlds on high;

Shall join the disembodied saints,
   And find its long-sought rest,
(That only bliss for which it pants,)
   In the Redeemer's breast.

2 In hope of that immortal crown,
   I now the cross sustain,
And gladly wander up and down,
   And smile at toil and pain:
I suffer on my threescore years,
   Till my Deliverer come,
And wipe away his servant's tears,
   And take his exile home.

3 Oh, what hath Jesus done for me!—
   Before my raptured eyes
Rivers of life divine I see,
   And trees of paradise!
I see a world of spirits bright,
   Who taste the pleasures there;
They are all robed in spotless white,
   And conquering palms they bear.

4 Oh, what are all my sufferings here,
   If, Lord, thou count me meet
With that enraptured host to appear,
   And worship at thy feet?
Give joy or grief, give ease or pain,
   Take life or friends away;
But let me find them all again
   In that eternal day.

252   C. M.   *Songs of Zion.*
Longing for Home.

O Land of rest, for thee I sigh!
   When will the moment come
When I shall lay my armor by
   And dwell in peace at home?

2 No tranquil joys on earth I know,
   No peaceful sheltering dome:
The world's a wilderness of wo;
   This world is not my home.

3 To Jesus Christ I fled for rest;
   He bade me cease to roam,
And lean for succor on his breast,
   And he'd conduct me home.

4 I would at once have quit the field
   Where foes with fury foam,
But, ah! my passport was not sealed;
   I could not yet go home.

5 When, by affliction sharply tried,
   I view the gaping tomb,
Although I dread death's chilling tide,
   Yet still I sigh for home.

6 Weary of wandering round and round
   This vale of sin and gloom,
I long to quit the unhallowed ground
   And dwell with Christ at home.

FAITH.

253   C. M.   *Watts.*

Faith of Things Unseen.—Heb. xi. 1, 3, 8, 10.

FAITH is the brightest evidence
  Of things beyond our sight,
Breaks through the clouds of flesh and sense,
  And dwells in heavenly light.

2 It sets times past in present view,
    Brings distant prospects home,
  Of things a thousand years ago,
    Or thousand years to come.

3 By faith we know the worlds were made
    By God's almighty word;
  Abram, to unknown countries led,
    By faith obeyed the Lord.

4 He sought a city fair and high,
    Built by the eternal hands,
  And faith assures us, though we die,
    That heavenly building stands.

254   L. M.   *Watts.*

We walk by Faith, not by Sight.

'TIS by the faith of joys to come
  We walk through deserts dark as night;
Till we arrive at heaven, our home,
  Faith is our guide, and faith our light.

The want of sight she well supplies;
  She makes the pearly gates appear;
Far into distant worlds she pries,
  And brings eternal glories near.

3 Cheerful we tread the desert through,
  While faith inspires a heavenly ray,
Though lions roar and tempests blow,
  And rocks and dangers fill the way.

4 So Abram, by divine command,
  Left his own house to walk with God;
His faith beheld the promised land,
  And fired his zeal along the road.

255   L. M. *Christian Psalmist.*

AS body when the soul has fled,
  As barren trees, decayed and dead,
Is faith: a hopeless, lifeless thing,
If not of righteous deeds, the spring.

2 One cup of healing oil and wine,
  One tear-drop shed on mercy's shrine,
Is thrice more grateful, Lord, to thee,
Than lifted eye, or bended knee.

3 In true, and heaven-born faith, we trace
  The source of every Christian grace;
Within the pious heart it plays,
A living fount of joy and praise.

4 Kind deeds of peace and love betray,
  Where'er the stream has found its way;

But where these spring not rich and fair,
The stream has never wandered there.

356   S. M.   *Beddome.*
Faith, its Author and Preciousness.—Eph. ii. 8.

FAITH !—'tis a precious grace
  Where'er it is bestowed !
It boasts of a celestial birth,
  And is the gift of God !

2 Jesus it owns a King,
  An all-atoning Priest :
It claims no merit of its own,
  But looks for all in Christ.

3 To him it leads the soul,
  When filled with deep distress,
Flies to the fountain of his blood,
  And trusts his righteousness.

4 Since 'tis thy work alone,
  And that divinely free !
Lord, send the Spirit of thy Son
  To work this faith in me !

HOPE.

257   C. M.   *Coombes.*
Flying to Christ under Trouble.—Heb. vi. 18.

IN all my troubles, sharp and strong,
  My soul to Jesus flies ;

My anchor, hope, is firm in him
  When swelling billows rise.

His comforts bear my spirits up;
  I trust a faithful God;
The sure foundation of my hope
  Is in a Savior's blood.

3 Loud hallelujahs sing, my soul,
  To thy Redeemer's name;
In joy, in sorrow, life, and death,
  His love is still the same.

258   L. M.
Hope in God.

THE God of my salvation lives;
  My nobler life he will sustain;
His word immortal vigor gives,
  Nor shall my glorious hope be vain.

2 Thy presence, Lord, can cheer my heart,
  Though every earthly comfort die;
Thy smile can bid my pains depart
  And raise my sacred pleasures high.

3 Oh, let me hear thy blissful voice,
  Inspiring life and joy divine;
The barren desert shall rejoice;
  'Tis paradise, if thou art mine.

259   S. M. (Abridged.)   *Toplady.*
Weak Believers Encouraged.—Ps. xxvii. 14.

YOUR harps, ye trembling saints,
  Down from the willows take:

Loud to the praise of love divine
    Bid every string awake.

2 Though in a foreign land,
    We are not far from home;
And nearer to our house above
    We every moment come.

2 His grace will to the end
    Stronger and brighter shine;
Nor present things, nor things to come,
    Shall quench the love divine.

4 [Fastened within the veil,
    Hope be our anchor strong;
His loving Spirit the sweet gale
    That wafts you smooth along.]

5 Wait till the shadows flee;
    Wait thy appointed hour;
Wait till the bridegroom of thy soul,
    Reveals his love with power.

6 The time of love will come;
    Then we shall clearly see,
Not only that he shed his blood,
    But each shall say, "FOR ME."

LOVE TO GOD.

260   C. M. (Abridged.)   *Doddridge.*
Lovest thou me? Feed my Lambs.—John xxi. 15.

Do not I love thee, O my Lord?
　Behold my heart and see;
And turn each cursed idol out
　That dares to rival thee.

2 Do not I love thee from my soul?
　Then let me nothing love;
Dead be my heart to every joy,
　When Jesus cannot move.

3 Is not thy name melodious still
　To my attentive ear?
Doth not each pulse with pleasure bound
　My Savior's voice to hear?

4 Thou knowest I love thee, dearest Lord;
　But, oh! I long to soar
Far from the sphere of mortal joys,
　And learn to love thee more.

261   7s.   *Cowper.*
Lovest Thou Me?—John xxi. 16.

Hark, my soul! it is the Lord;
'Tis thy Savior, hear his word;

Jesus speaks, and speaks to thee:
"Say, poor sinner, lovest thou me?

2 "I delivered thee when bound,
And when wounded, healed thy wound;
Sought thee wandering, set thee right,
Turned thy darkness into light.

3 "Can a woman's tender care
Cease toward the child she bare?
Yes, she may forgetful be:
Yet will I remember thee.

4 "Mine is an unchanging love,
Higher than the heights above,
Deeper than the depths beneath,
Free and faithful, strong as death.

5 "Thou shalt see my glory soon,
When the work of grace is done;
Partner of my throne shalt be:
Say, poor sinner, lovest thou me?"

6 Lord, it is my chief complaint,
That my love is weak and faint;
Yet I love thee, and adore;
Oh for grace to love thee more!

262 L. M. *Kent.*
The Banquet of Love.—Can. ii. 4.

TO banquet once the spouse was led
By Him who for her pardon bled;

There was her soul indulged to prove
His looks divine and banner love.

2 Like her, my soul, beneath the word,
Was led to banquet with my Lord:
His flesh I ate, his love I sung,
While o'er my head his banner hung.

3 'Twas then I found a heaven within,
And pardoning blood for every sin,
While love eternal, great, and free,
Was still his banner over me.

4 Thus in his favor life I found
Whose temples once with thorns were crown'd
While o'er my head, a wretch depraved,
In folds of love his banner waved.

5 Oh, sweet repast of living bread:
"Here let me die, my Lord," I said;
"I'm sick of love, and faint to see
Thy banner thus spread over me."

6 "'Twas for thy sin, my love," he said,
"Those poignant thorns surround my head;
I groaned and bled on Calvary's tree
To spread this banner over thee."

7 Jesus, when thou shall call, I'll fly
To join the marriage-feast on high,
And o'er thy glorious fulness rove,
And pay my Savior love for love.

LOVE TO GOD.

263   L. M.   *Watts.*

Religion vain without Love.—1 Cor. xiii. 1, 9.

HAD I the tongues of Greeks and Jews,
And nobler speech than angels use,
If love be absent, I am found,
Like tinkling brass, an empty sound.

2 Were I inspired to preach and tell
All that is done in heaven and hell,
Or could my faith the world remove,
Still I am nothing without love.

3 Should I distribute all my store
To feed the bowels of the poor,
Or give my body to the flame
To gain a martyr's glorious name.

4 If love to God and love to men
Be absent, all my hopes are vain;
Nor tongues, nor gifts, nor fiery zeal,
The works of love can e'er fulfil.

BROTHERLY LOVE.

264   S. M.   *Fawcett.*

Love to the Brethren.

BLEST be the tie that binds
Our hearts in Christian love:
The fellowship of kindred minds
Is like to that above.

BROTHERLY LOVE.

2 Before our Father's throne
   We pour our ardent prayers;
Our fears, our hopes, our aims, are one,
   Our comforts and our cares.

3 We share our mutual woes,
   Our mutual burdens bear,
And often for each other flows
   The sympathizing tear.

4 When we asunder part,
   It gives us inward pain,
But we shall still be joined in heart,
   And hope to meet again.

5 This glorious hope revives
   Our courage by the way,
While each in expectation lives,
   And longs to see the day.

6 From sorrow, toil, and pain,
   And sin, we shall be free,
And perfect love and friendship reign
   Through all eternity.

265   C. M.   *Watts.*
Brotherly Love.—Ps. cxxxiii.

LO! what an entertaining sight
   Are brethren that agree,
Brethren whose cheerful hearts unite
   In bands of piety!

2 When streams of love from Christ the spring
    Descend to every soul,
And heavenly peace, with balmy wing,
    Shades and bedews the whole.

3 'Tis like the oil, divinely sweet,
    On Aaron's reverend head;
The trickling drops perfumed his feet,
    And o'er his garments spread.

4 'Tis pleasant as the morning dews
    That fall on Zion's hill,
Where God his mildest glory shows,
    And makes his grace distil.

266   S. M.   *Vanmeter.*
Brotherly Love.

BOUND by the cords of love,
    As kindred we unite;
And sing the praise of him above,
    With infinite delight!

2 Heirs of the same estate,
    The subjects of one King:
The tie of union is so sweet,
    It tunes our voice to sing.

3 We pledge our heart and hand,
    This union to maintain
While traveling through this barren land
    Of sorrow, toil and pain.

4 As branches of one Vine;
    As members of one Head:

BROTHERLY LOVE.

Sustained alike, by heavenly wine,
  And by one living bread.

5 We know each other's voice,
    While wading through the deep:
  "Rejoice with those that do rejoice,
    And weep with those that weep."

6 Though we must bid adieu,
    And heave the parting sigh;
  We hope this union to renew
    In fairer worlds on high!

7 Encouraged by this hope,
    We'll patiently endure,
  Till all our pains are swallowed up,
    On heaven's delightful shore!

267　　　　　8s.　　　　　*Baldwin*
Union of Saints.

FROM whence does this union arise,
    That hatred is conquered by love?
  It fastens our souls with such ties
    That distance nor time can remove.

2 It cannot in Eden be found,
    Nor yet in a Paradise lost;
  It grows on Immanuel's ground,
    And Jesus' dear blood it did cost.

3 My friends all so dear are to me,
    Our souls so united in love,

Where Jesus is gone we shall be,
In yonder blest mansions above.

4 Oh, why then so loath now to part,
Since we shall ere long meet again?
Engraved on Immanuel's heart,
At a distance we cannot remain.

THE CHURCH.

268   L. M.   *Watts.*
God the Glory and Defence of Zion.

HAPPY the church, thou sacred place,
The seat of thy Creator's grace;
Thy holy courts are his abode,
Thou earthly palace of our God.

2 Thy walls are strength, and at thy gates
A guard of heavenly warriors waits;
Nor shall thy deep foundations move,
Fixed on his counsels and his love.

3 Thy foes in vain designs engage,
Against his throne in vain they rage;
Like rising waves with angry roar,
That dash and die upon the shore.

4 Then let us still in Zion dwell;
Nor fear the wrath of earth and hell;
His arms embrace this happy ground,
Like brazen bulwarks built around.

5 God is our shield, and God our sun;
Swift as the fleeting moments run,
On us he sheds new beams of grace,
And we reflect his brightest praise.

269 L. M. *Kent.*
Zion, the City of God.

ZION'S a city God hath blest
With peace and everlasting rest,—
A glorious city, strong and fair:
Jehovah dwells forever there.

2 Her ancient walls appear to be
The workmanship of Deity;
Founded in grace they still appear
Without a flaw or chasm there.

3 Oft has this city's strength been tried
By desperate foes on every side:
But all in vain the attempts have been:
She baffles all the assaults of sin.

4 Count ye her towers, how high they rise,
Her golden spires, they pierce the skies;
Her golden streets are fair to view,
Her palaces and bulwarks too.

5 Then round her walk, her turrets tell,
Mark all her brazen bulwarks well;
Spread far and wide her deathless fame,
Her pearly gates and walls of flame.

6 Her founder's love has ever proved,
Like Salem's mounts, which ne'er were moved;

'Tis fixed on this eternal base,
The grace of God, and gift by grace.

270   7s, 6s.   *Vanmeter.*
Mount Zion.—Ps. 48, 2.

BEHOLD! the mount of Zion!
　The City of our God!
The beauty of creation,
　And place of his abode:
Christ is the great foundation
　On which this building stands;
He reared, for his own glory,
　This temple without hands.

2 Through everlasting ages,
　This house shall stand secure;
The Lord, for it engages
　His wisdom, love and power;
Nor shall the hosts of Satan
　Against it e'er prevail;
Though kingdoms be demolished,
　And heaven and earth should fail.

3 The Rock, on which it's founded,
　Will last without decay;
With walls it is surrounded,
　Which guard it every way.
Each stone is wisely polished,
　And fitted to its place;
And all are well cemented
　With God's redeeming grace.

4 Nor storms, nor persecutions,
　　Shall ever beat it down;
　Nor floods of tribulation
　　Shall move a single stone.
　With Christ they all shall triumph
　　O'er sin, and death, and hell;
　And with him, in his glory,
　　They shall forever dwell.

271   C. M.   *Watts.*
　　Going to Church.—Ps. cxxii.

HOW did my heart rejoice to hear
　　My friends devoutly say,
"In Zion let us all appear,
　　And keep the solemn day!"

2 I love her gates, I love the road:
　　The church, adorned with grace,
　Stands like a palace built for God
　　To show his milder face.

3 Up to her courts, with joys unknown,
　　The holy tribes repair;
　The Son of David holds his throne
　　And sits in judgment there.

4 He hears our praises and complaints,
　　And, while his awful voice
　Divides the sinners from the saints,
　　We tremble and rejoice.

5 Peace be within this sacred place,
　　And joy a constant guest!

THE CHURCH.

With holy gifts and heavenly grace
Be her attendants blest!

6 My soul shall pray for Zion still,
While life or breath remains;
There my best friends, my kindred, dwell,
There God my Savior reigns.

272   S. M.   *Presby. Selec.*
Love to The Church.

I LOVE thy kingdom, Lord,
The house of thine abode;
The church our blest Redeemer saved
With his own precious blood.

2 I love thy church, O God!
Her walls before thee stand
Dear as the apple of thine eye,
And graven on thy hand.

3 If e'er to bless thy sons
My voice or hands deny,
These hands let useful skill forsake,
This voice in silence die.

4 If e'er my heart forget
Her welfare or her woe,
Let every joy this heart forsake,
And every grief o'erflow.

5 For her my tears shall fall,
For her my prayers ascend;
To her my cares and toils be given,
Till toils and cares shall end.

6 Beyond my highest joy
   I prize her heavenly ways,
 Her sweet communion, solemn vows,
   Her hymns of love and praise.

273 L. M. (Abridged) *Watts.*
The Church the Garden of Christ.—Sol. Song,
iv. 12, 13, 15; and v. 1.

WE are a garden walled around,
   Chosen and made peculiar ground;
 A little spot enclosed by grace
 Out of the world's wide wilderness.

2 Like trees of myrrh and spice we stand,
  Planted by God the Father's hand;
  And all his springs in Zion flow
  To make the young plantation grow.

3 Awake, O heavenly wind, and come,
  Blow on this garden of perfume;
  Spirit divine, descend, and breathe
  A gracious gale on plants beneath.

4 Make our best spices flow abroad
  To entertain our Savior-God;
  And faith, and love, and joy appear,
  And every grace be active here.

274 P. M. *Christian Psalmist.*
House of the Lord.

YOU may sing of the beauty of mountain and dale,
   Of the silvery streamlet and flowers of the vale;
 But the place most delightful this earth can afford,
 Is the place of devotion—the house of the Lord.

2 You may boast of the sweetness of day's early dawn—
Of the sky's softening graces when the day is just gone;
But there's no other season or time can compare
With the hour of devotion—the season of prayer.

3 You may value the friendships of youth and of age,
And select for your comrades the noble and sage;
But the friends that most cheer me on life's rugged road,
Are the friends of my Master—the children of God.

4 You may talk of your prospects, of fame, or of wealth,
And the hopes that oft flatter the favorites of health;
But the hope of bright glory—of heavenly bliss!
Take away every other, and give me but this.

5 Ever hail, blessed temple, abode of my Lord!
I will turn to thee often, to hear from his word;
I will walk to the altar with those that I love,
And delight in the prospects revealed from above.

275   8, 7, (Abridged.)   *Newton.*
Zion's Increase prayed for.—Ps. lxxxv. 6.

SAVIOR, visit thy plantation;
  Grant us, Lord, a gracious rain;
All will come to desolation
  Unless thou return again:
    Lord, revive us,
  All our help must come from thee.

2 Keep no longer at a distance;
  Shine upon us, from on high,
Lest, for want of thine assistance,
  Every plant should droop and die: Lord, etc.

3 Surely once thy garden flourished,
  Every part looked gay and green;
Then thy word our spirits nourished,
  Happy seasons we have seen: Lord, etc.

4 But a drought has since succeeded,
    And a sad decline we see;
Lord, thy help is greatly needed,
    Help can only come from thee: Lord, etc.

5 Where are those we counted leaders,
    Filled with zeal, and love, and truth?
Old professors, tall as cedars,
    Bright examples to our youth! Lord, etc.

6 Some in whom we once delighted,
    We shall meet no more below;
Some, alas, we fear are blighted,
    Scarce a single leaf they show; Lord, etc.

7 Younger plants—the sight how pleasant!—
    Covered thick with blossoms stood;
But they cause us grief at present,
    Frosts have nipped them in the bud: Lord, etc.

8 Dearest Savior, hasten hither,
    Thou canst make them bloom again,
Oh, permit them not to wither,
    Let not all our hopes be vain: Lord, etc.

9 Let our mutual love be fervent;
    Make us prevalent in prayers;
Let each one esteemed thy servant
    Shun the world's bewitching snares: Lord, etc.

10 Break the tempter's fatal power.
    Turn the stony heart to flesh,
And begin from this good hour
    To revive thy work afresh: Lord, etc.

RECEPTION OF MEMBERS.

276   C. M.   *Watts.*

Not ashamed of the Gospel.—2 Tim. i. 12.

I'M not ashamed to own my Lord,
   Or to defend his cause,
Maintain the honor of his word,
   The glory of his cross.

2 Jesus, my God, I know his name,
   His name is all my trust,
Nor will he put my soul to shame,
   Nor let my hope be lost.

3 Firm as his throne his promise stands,
   And he can well secure
What I've committed to his hands
   Till the decisive hour.

4 Then will he own my worthless name
   Before his Father's face,
And in the New Jerusalem
   Appoint my soul a place.

277   C. M.   *Watts.*

The Hope of Heaven our Support under Trials.

WHEN I can read my title clear
   To mansions in the skies,
I'll bid farewell to every fear,
   And wipe my weeping eyes.

2 Should earth against my soul engage,
   And hellish darts be hurled,
Then I can smile at Satan's rage,
   And face a frowning world.

3 Let cares like a wild deluge come,
   And storms of sorrow fall,
May I but safely reach my home,
   My God, my heaven, my all.

4 There shall I bathe my weary soul
   In seas of heavenly rest,
And not a wave of trouble roll
   Across my peaceful breast.

273   S. M.   *Muhlenberg.*
The Ark of Safety.

LIKE Noah's weary dove,
   That soared the earth around,
But not a resting-place above
   The cheerless waters found:

2 Oh, cease, my wandering soul,
   On restless wing to roam;
All the wide world, to either pole,
   Has not for thee a home.

3 Behold the Ark of God,
   Behold the open door;
Hasten to gain that dear abode,
   And rove, my soul, no more.

4 There safe thou shalt abide,
   There sweet shall be thy rest,

And every longing satisfied,
  With full salvation blessed.

And when the waves of ire
  Again the earth shall fill,
The Ark shall ride the sea of fire,
  Then rest on Zion's hill.

79 7s. *Christian Psalmist.*

PEOPLE of the living God,
  I have sought the world around,
Paths of sin and sorrow trod,
  Peace and comfort nowhere found.

Now to you my spirit turns—
  Turns, a fugitive unblest;
Brethren, where your altar burns,
  Oh! receive me into rest.

Lonely, I no longer roam,
  Like the cloud, the wind, the wave,
Where you dwell shall be my home,
  Where you die, shall be my grave:

Mine the God whom you adore,
  Your Redeemer shall be mine;
Earth can fill my soul no more,
  Every idol I resign.

80 C. M. *(Altered.)*
Come in, thou Blessed of the Lord.—Gen. xxiv. 3.

COME in, ye blessed of our God,
  And join his children here;

Washed in the Savior's cleansing blood,
  For him, your Lord, appear.

2 Stay not within the wilderness,
   Nor waiting at the door;
 Sweet Jesus will your woes redress,
   Were they ten thousand more.

3 Though fearing, trembling, rise and come!
   Yield to the Savior's voice;
 For hungering, thirsting souls there's room;
   Oh, make the blissful choice!

4 Room in the Savior's gracious breast,—
   That breast which glows with love;
 Room in the church, his chosen rest,
   And room in heaven above.

5 Why will you longer lingering stay,
   When Jesus says, "there's room"?
 "Now is the time, the accepted day;"
   Arise! he bids you come!

281   P. M. (Abridged.)   *Dover's Sel*
         The Joy of Assurance.

HOW happy are they
   Who the Savior obey,
 And whose treasures are laid up above!
   Tongue cannot express
   The sweet comfort and peace
 Of a soul in its earliest love.

That comfort was mine
When the favor divine
I first found in the blood of the Lamb;
When my heart first believed,
Oh, what joy I received,
What a heaven in Jesus' name!

'Twas a heaven below
The Redeemer to know;
And the angels could do nothing more
Than to fall at his feet,
And the story repeat,
And the Savior of sinners adore.

Jesus, all the day long,
Was my joy and my song;
Oh, that all his salvation might see!
He hath loved me, I cried,
He hath suffered and died,
To redeem such a rebel as me.

What a mercy is this!
What a heaven of bliss!
How unspeakably favored am I,
Gathered into the fold,
With believers enrolled,
With believers to live and to die!

Now my remnant of days
Would I spend to His praise
Who hath died my poor soul to redeem;

Whether many or few,
All my years are his due:
May they all be devoted to him!

282   C. M.   *E. Jone*

The Successful Resolve.—Esther iv. 16.

COME, humble sinner, in whose breast
A thousand thoughts revolve,
Come, with your guilt and fear opprest,
And make this last resolve:

2 I'll go to Jesus, though my sin
Hath like a mountain rose;
I know his courts, I'll enter in,
Whatever may oppose.

3 Prostrate I'll lie before his throne,
And there my guilt confess;
I'll tell him I'm a wretch undone,
Without his sovereign grace.

4 I'll to the gracious King approach,
Whose scepter pardon gives;
Perhaps he may command my touch,
And then the suppliant lives.

5 Perhaps he will admit my plea,
Perhaps will hear my prayer;
But if I perish I will pray,
And perish only there.

6 I can but perish if I go,
I am resolved to try;

For if I stay away, I know
I must forever die.

283　　　　11, 8,　　　　*Vanmeter.*
"*My Grace is Sufficient for Thee.*"—2 Cor. xii. 9.

DESPONDING believer, come, hold up thy head,
　Though many thy troubles may be;
For Jesus, thy Savior, hath promised and said:
　"My grace is sufficient for thee."

2 Though Satan may tempt thee, and buffet thee sore,
　Yet he, at his bidding, shall flee;
Possessing on earth and in heaven all power,
　" His grace is sufficient for thee."

3 The Lord will uphold thee, and cause thee to stand,
　While on the tempestuous sea;
And 'midst all thy troubles and trials on land,
　" His grace is sufficient for thee."

4 The world may forsake thee, and set thee at naught;
　Rejoice when thy troubles they see;
Yet Jesus still loves the dear sheep he has bought:
　" His grace is sufficient for thee."

5 And when thou shalt sink into death's cold embrace,
　And earthly assistance shall flee;
His boundless, redeeming unmerited grace,
　Will then be sufficient for thee.

284　　　　L. M.　　　　*Vanmeter.*
Leaving all for Christ.

"IF ye love me," says Christ, the Lord,
　"Keep my commandments and my word:
Take up your cross and follow me,
And ye shall my disciples be.

2 "Except a man, himself deny,
  Of worldly lusts and vanity,
  Forego the world's abuse and shame,
  He is not worthy of my name.

3 "He must esteem my riches more
  Than hills of wealth laid up in store:
  His consort and his friends forsake,
  If he would of my joys partake.

4 "He that will for his Savior leave
  The world, shall in this life receive
  A hundred fold, and shall enjoy
  Eternal life with him on high."

BAPTISM.

285　　　　　S. M.　　　　　*Daniel.*
Christ's Baptism an Example for us.

THE glorious Son of God
　To John the Baptist came,
Went meekly into Jordan's stream,
　And was immersed by him.

2 Let each believer view
　This blest example given,
And prove their love of his commands
　And follow him to heaven.

286　　　　　C. M.　　　　　*Stennett.*
Immersion.

THUS was the great Redeemer plunged
　In Jordan's swelling flood,

BAPTISM. 265

    To show he must be soon baptised
      In tears, and sweat, and blood.

2 Thus was his sacred body laid
    Beneath the yielding wave:
Thus was his sacred body raised
    Out of the liquid grave.

3 Lord, we thy precepts would obey,
    In thy own footsteps tread,
Would die, be buried, rise with thee,
    Our ever-living Head.

287 L. M. *Daniel.*
Primitive Practice Perpetuated.

WHAT lovely band is this I see,
    All singing in sweet harmony,
Uniting round the water-side,
And praising Jesus crucified?

2 These are the followers of the Lamb;
Here they are come to own his name;
Their humble strains ascend the skies;
In faith they're come to be baptised.

3 This brings to view the ancient days,
When first the gospel church was raised,
No other mode was then devised:
Believing souls were thus baptised:

4 Baptised into the Savior's death,
Arising, lived the life of faith:
Giving to Christ, the Lord, the praise,
By walking in his humble ways.

288   C. M.   *Anon.*

Why tarriest thou? arise, and be baptized.—Acts xxii. 16.

BELIEVING soul, "Why tarriest thou!
   Arise, and be baptised;"
Yield to the word; to Jesus bow;
   Let pride be sacrificed.

2 Buried in baptism with our God,
   We bid the world adieu;
Rising like him from Jordan's flood,
   Begin our lives anew.

3 Ye gilded vanities, depart,
   With all your flattering charms;
I clasp my Savior to my heart,
   He folds me in his arms.

4 Oh, may thine arms, Almighty Lord,
   Support me through the way,
And, while I thus thy grace record,
   Let sin be washed away.

289   C. M.

Baptism.—Matt. iii. 13, 17.

DEAR Lord! and will thy pardoning love
   Embrace a wretch so vile?
Wilt thou my load of guilt remove.
   And bless me with thy smile?

2 Hast thou the cross for me endured,
   And all its shame despised?

And shall I be ashamed, O Lord,
With thee to be baptised?

3 Didst thou the great example lead
In Jordan's swelling flood?
And shall my pride disdain the deed
That's worthy of my God?

4 Dear Lord, the ardor of thy love
Reproves my cold delays;
And now my willing footsteps move
In thy delightful ways!

290   L. M.   *Gadsby's Col.*
"*Can any man forbid water,*" &c.—Acts x. 47.

COME, ye beloved of the Lord,
Behold the Lamb, the incarnate Word;
He died and rose again for you!
What more could your Redeemer do?

2 We to this place are come to show
What we to boundless mercy owe;
The Savior's footsteps to explore,
And tread the path he trod before.

291   L. M. *(Altered by B. Francis.)*
Not ashamed of Christ.

JESUS, and shall it ever be,
A mortal man ashamed of thee!
Ashamed of thee, whom angels praise,
Whose glories rise through endless days.

BAPTISM.

2 Ashamed of Jesus! sooner far
Let evening blush to own a star;
He sheds the beams of light divine
O'er this benighted soul of mine.

3 Ashamed of Jesus! just as soon
Let midnight be ashamed of noon;
'Tis midnight with my soul, till he,
Bright morning Star! bid darkness flee.

4 Ashamed of Jesus! that dear friend
On whom my hopes of heaven depend:
No; when I blush, be this my shame.
That I no more revere his name.

5 Ashamed of Jesus! yes, I may,
When I've no guilt to wash away,
No tear to wipe, no good to crave,
No fears to quell, no soul to save.

6 Till then—nor is my boasting vain—
Till then I boast a Savior slain!
And oh, may this my glory be
That Christ is not ashamed of me!

292 8s, 7s. *Christian Psalmist.*

JESUS, I my cross have taken,
  All to leave, and follow thee;
Friendless, poor, despised, forsaken,
  Thou, from hence, my all shalt be.
Perish, every fond ambition,

All I've sought, or hoped, or known ;
Yet how rich is my condition.
God and heaven are still my own.

2 Let the world despise and leave me ;
They have left my Savior too :
Human hearts and looks deceive me ;
Thou art not, like them untrue ;
And while thou shalt smile upon me ;
God of wisdom, love and might,
Foes may hate and friends disown me ;
Show thy face, and all is bright.

THE LORD'S SUPPER.

293   L. M. (Abridged.) *Watts.*
The Lord's Supper Instituted.—1 Cor. xi. 23.

'TWAS on that dark, that doleful night.
When powers of earth and hell arose
Against the Son of God's delight,
And friends betrayed him to his foes.

2 Before the mournful scene began,
He took the bread, and blessed and brake:
What love through all his actions ran !
What wondrous words of grace he spake !

3 " This is my body, broke for sin ;
Receive, and eat the living food ;"
Then took the cup and blessed the wine ;
" 'Tis the new covenant in my blood."

4 " Do this," he cried, " till time shall end,
  In memory of your dying friend;
Meet at my table, and record
  The love of your departed Lord."

5 [Jesus, thy feast we celebrate,
  We show thy death, we sing thy name.
Till thou return, and we shall eat
  The marriage-supper of the Lamb.]

294.   C. M.   *Watts.*
Divine Love making a Feast, &c. — Luke xiv. 17, 23.

HOW sweet and awful is the place
  With Christ within the doors,
While everlasting love displays
  The choicest of her stores!

2 Here every bowel of our God
    With soft compassion rolls;
  Here peace and pardon, bought with blood,
    Is food for dying souls.

3 [While all our hearts and all our songs
    Join to admire the feast,
  Each of us cry, with thankful tongues,
    "Lord, why was I a guest!"

4 "Why was I made to hear thy voice,
    And enter while there's room,
  When thousands make a wretched choice,
    And rather starve than come?"

5 'Twas the same love that spread the feast
    That sweetly forced us in,
Else we had still refused to taste,
    And perished in our sin.

295   L. M. (Abridged.)   *Watts.*

Incomparable Food; or, the Flesh and Blood of Christ.

WE sing the amazing deeds
    That grace divine performs;
The eternal God comes down and bleeds
    To nourish dying worms.

2   This soul-reviving wine,
    Dear Savior, 'tis thy blood;
We thank that sacred flesh of thine
    For this immortal food.

3   The banquet that we eat
    Is made of heavenly things;
Earth hath no dainties half so sweet
    As our Redeemer brings.

4   The angelic host above
    Can never taste this food,
They feast upon their Maker's love,
    But not a Savior's blood.

5   Come, all ye drooping saints,
    And banquet with the King,
This wine will drown your sad complaints
    And tune your voice to sing.

THE LORD'S SUPPER.

296   C. M.   *Stennett.*

Eat, O Friends!—Cant. v, 1.

LORD, at thy table I behold
   The wonders of thy grace,
But most of all admire that I
   Should find a welcome place.

2 I, that am all defiled with sin,
   A rebel to my God;
I, that have crucified his Son,
   And trampled on his blood.

3 What strange, surprising grace is this,
   That such a soul has room!
My Savior takes me by the hand.
   My Jesus bids me come.

4 "Eat, O my friends!" the Savior cries;
   "The feast was made for you;
For you I groaned, and bled, and died,
   And rose, and triumphed too!"

5 With trembling faith and bleeding hearts,
   Lord, we accept thy love;
'Tis a rich banquet we have had:
   What will it be above!

6 Ye saints below and hosts of heaven,
   Join all your praising powers;
No theme is like redeeming love,
   No Savior is like ours.

THE LORD'S SUPPER.

297 C. M. *Christian Psalmist.*

THE King of heaven his table spreads,
  And blessings crown the board;
Not paradise with all its joys,
  Could such delight afford.

2 Pardon and peace to dying men,
  And endless life are given,
Through the rich blood that Jesus shed,
  To raise our souls to heaven.

3 Millions of souls, in glory now,
  Were fed and feasted here;
And millions more, still on the way,
  Around the board appear.

4 All things are ready, come away,
  Nor weak excuses frame;
Crowd to your places at the feast,
  And bless the Founder's name.

298 L. M. *Christian Psalmist.*

HOW pleasing to behold and see
  The friends of Jesus all agree,
To sit around his sacred board
As members of one common Lord.

2 Here we behold the dawn of bliss—
Here we enjoy the Savior's grace—
Here we behold his precious blood,
Which sweetly pleads for us with God.

3 While here we sit, we would implore
That love may spread from shore to shore.

'Till all the saints like us combine
To praise the Lord in songs divine.

299   L. M.   *Watts.*
Remember Jesus.—Luke xxii. 10.

THE Lord of life his table spread,
With his own flesh and dying blood:
We on the rich provisions feed,
And taste the wine, and bless our God!

2 May sinful sweets be all forgot,
And earth grow less in our esteem;
Christ and his love fill every thought,
And faith and hope be fixed on him.

300   L. M.   *Parkinson's Selec.*
Godly Sorrow for Sin.

PITY a helpless sinner, Lord,
Who would believe thy gracious word,
But own my heart with shame and grief,
A sink of sin and unbelief.

2 Lord, in thy house I read there's room,
And, venturing hard, behold, I come!
But can there, tell me, can there be
Among thy children room for me?

3 I eat the bread and drink the wine,
But ah! my soul wants more than sign:
I faint unless I feed on thee,
And drink thy blood as shed for me.

4 For sinners, Lord, thou camest to bleed,
And I'm a sinner, vile indeed!
Lord, I believe thy grace is free;
Oh, magnify that grace in me!

BEFORE PREACHING.

301   L. M. (Abridged.)   *Watts.*
The Enjoyment of Christ; or, Delight in Worship.

FAR from my thoughts, vain world, begone,
  Let my religious hours alone:
Fain would my eyes my Savior see,
I wait a visit, Lord, from thee.

2 My heart grows warm with holy fire,
And kindles with a pure desire:
Come, my dear Jesus, from above,
And feed my soul with heavenly love.

3 Blessed Jesus, what delicious fare!
How sweet thy entertainments are!
Never did angels taste above
Redeeming grace and dying love.

4 Hail, great Immanuel, all divine,
In thee thy Father's glories shine;
Thou brightest, sweetest, fairest one,
That eyes have seen or angels known.

302   L. M.   *Watts.*
The same.

I SEND the joys of earth away,
  Away ye tempters of the mind,
False as the smooth, deceitful sea,
And empty as the whistling wind.

2 Your streams were floating me along
Down to the gulf of dark despair,

And whilst I listened to your song,
Your streams had e'en conveyed me there.

3 Lord, I adore thy matchless grace,
That warned me of that dark abyss,
That drew me from those treacherous seas,
And bid me seek superior bliss.

4 Now to the shining realms above
I stretch my hands and glance my eyes;
O for the pinions of a dove
To bear me to the upper skies!

5 There from the bosom of my God
Oceans of endless pleasure roll;
There would I fix my last abode,
And drown the sorrows of my soul.

303　　　　C. M.　　　　*Hart.*
The same.—Cant. iv. 16.

ONCE more we come before our God
Once more his blessing ask;
O, may not duty seem a load
Nor worship prove a task.

2 Father, thy quickening Spirit send
From heaven, in Jesus' name,
To make our waiting minds attend,
And put our souls in frame.

3 May we receive the word we hear,
Each in an honest heart;
Hoard up the precious treasure there,
And never with it part.

4 To seek thee all our hearts dispose;
   To each thy blessings suit;
And let the seed thy servant sows
   Produce a copious fruit.

5 Bid the refreshing north wind wake,
   Say to the south wind, Blow;
Let every plant the power partake,
   And all the garden grow.

6 Revive the parched with heavenly showers;
   The cold with warmth divine;
And as the benefit is ours,
   Be all the glory thine.

304   S. M.   *Vanmeter.*

Invoking the Holy Spirit.—See Luke xi, 13.

COME, Holy Spirit, come,
   And give us light divine;
Remove our doubts, dispel our gloom,
   And on our darkness shine.

2 Help our infirmities,
   And teach us how to pray;
And give the children large supplies
   Of heavenly food to-day.

3 Console each troubled heart,
   And make the feeble strong;
Warm our affections, and impart
   Devotion to each tongue.

4 Thy holy unction give,
   To him that sows the seed;

And may our hearts the word receive,
And on its dainties feed.

305　　　　C. M.　　　　*Watts.*
The Holy Spirit Invoked.

COME, Holy Spirit, heavenly Dove,
With all thy quickening powers,
Kindle a flame of sacred love
In these cold hearts of ours.

2 Look, how we grovel here below,
Fond of these trifling toys;
Our souls can neither fly nor go,
To reach eternal joys.

3 In vain we tune our formal songs,
In vain we strive to rise;
Hosannas languish on our tongues,
And our devotion dies.

4 Dear Lord! and shall we ever live
At this poor, dying rate?
Our love so faint, so cold to thee,
And thine to us so great!

5 Come, Holy Spirit, heavenly Dove,
With all thy quickening powers,
Come, shed abroad a Saviour's love,
And that shall kindle ours.

306　　　　L. M.　　　　*Stowell.*
The Mercy-Seat.

FROM every stormy wind that blows,
From every swelling tide of woes,

There is a calm, a sure retreat:
'Tis found beneath the Mercy-Seat.

2 There is a place where Jesus sheds
The oil of gladness on our heads;
A place of all on earth most sweet:
It is the blood-bought Mercy-Seat.

3 There is a scene where spirits blend,
Where friend holds fellowship with friend,
Though sundered far: by faith they meet
Around one common Mercy-Seat.

4 Ah! whither could we flee for aid,
When tempted, desolate, dismayed,—
Or how the hosts of hell defeat,
Had suffering saints no Mercy-Seat.

5 There, *there*, on eagle-wings we soar,
And sin and sense seem all no more;
And heaven comes down our souls to greet,
And glory crowns the Mercy-Seat.

6 Oh, let my hand forget her skill,
My tongue be silent, cold and still,
This bounding heart forget to beat,
If I forget the Mercy-Seat.

307   7s.   *Leland.*
Meeting.

BRETHREN, I am come again,
Let us join to pray and sing;
Joseph lives and Jesus reigns,
Praise him in the highest strains.

2 Many days and weeks have past
Since we met together last;

Yet our lives do still remain,
Here on earth we meet again.

3 Many of our friends are gone
To their long eternal home;
We are waiting here below,
Soon we after them shall go.

4 Brethren, tell me how you do;
Does your love continue true?
Are you waiting for your King,
When he shall return again?

5 If you want to know of me,
How I am, or what I be;
Here I am, behold who will,
Sure I am a sinner still.

6 Weak and wounded, sick and lame,
All unholy, all unclean;
Worse and worse myself I see,
Yet the Lord remembers me.

308 C. M. *Vanmeter.*
The Broad and the Narrow Way.—Matth. vii. 13, 14.

BROAD is the road, and wide the gate,
That lead to death, where thousands meet:
But straight and narrow is the way,
That leads to life and endless day.

2 In these two roads, are all mankind,
Yet few this narrow way can find;
While thousands shun this narrow path,
And choose the road that leads to death

3 Behold! the pilgrim as he goes,
Meeting with sorrows, pains and woes,
And see the heedless multitude,
Treading, with ease, the downward road:

4 But oh! the difference in the end!
The wicked shall to hell descend!
While heaven, with its eternal joys,
Awaits the pilgrim when he dies!

309　　　　　C. M.　　　　*Vanmeter.*
Religion worth more than all else.

LET others compass seas and lands,
　To gather earthly toys;
Lord, may I follow thy commands,
　And seek for nobler joys.

2 Let kings and monarchs wear the crown,
　And lords in affluence live;
May I thy righteousness put on:
　Thy gracious smiles receive.

3 Whilst others seek for carnal wealth,
　And toil for golden ore;
Lord, grant my soul religious health,
　And I desire no more!

310　　　　　L. M.　　　　*Hart.*
Stony Heart.—Isa. lxiv. 1; Ezek. xi. 19.

O, FOR a glance of heavenly day,
To take this stubborn stone away,
And thaw, with beams of love divine,
This heart, this frozen heart of mine.

2 The rocks can rend: the earth can quake,
The seas can roar; the mountains shake:
Of feeling, all things show some sign,
But this unfeeling heart of mine.

3 To hear the sorrows thou hast felt,
Dear Lord, an adamant would melt!
But I can read each moving line,
And nothing moves this heart of mine.

4 Thy judgments, too, unmoved I hear,
(Amazing thought!) which devils fear:
Mercy and wrath in vain combine
To stir this stupid heart of mine.

5 But something yet can do the deed!
And that dear something much I need;
Thy Spirit can from dross refine,
And move and melt this heart of mine.

CLOSING HYMNS.

311 L. M. *Hart.*
Dismission.

DISMISS us with thy blessing, Lord,
Help us to feed upon thy word;
All that has been amiss forgive,
And let thy truth within us live.

2 Though we are guilty, thou art good,
Oh, wash us in the Savior's blood;
Give every fettered soul release,
And bid us all depart in peace.

CLOSING HYMNS.

312   8s, 7s.   *Newton.*
May the Grace, &c.—2 Cor. xiii. 42.

MAY the grace of Christ, our Savior,
    And the Father's boundless love,
With the Holy Spirit's favor,
    Rest upon us from above!

2 Thus may we abide in union
    With each other and the Lord;
And possess, in sweet communion
    Joys which earth cannot afford.

313   C. M.   *Vanmeter.*
Religion.

RELIGION! what a vast estate,
    On guilty worms bestowed!
Not all the riches of the great,
    Are worth this gift of God!

2 How transient is all earthly bliss!
    How poor is shining gold!
And mortal crowns, compared with this,
    How worthless to behold!

3 In all things else let me be crossed:
    Lord, give this pearl to me!
Without it I'm forever lost,
    To all eternity!

314   L. M.   *Watts.*
Praise to God from all Nations.

FROM all that dwell below the skies
    Let the Creator's praise arise;

Let the Redeemer's name be sung
Through every land, by every tongue.
2 Eternal are thy mercies, Lord;
Eternal truth attends thy word;
Thy praise shall sound from shore to shore
Till earth and time shall be no more.

315   7s.   *Masters.*
Religion.

'TIS religion that can give
  Sweetest pleasures while we live;
'Tis religion must supply
Solid comfort when we die.
2 After death its joys will be
Lasting as eternity!
Be the living God my friend,
Then my bliss shall never end.

316   C. M.   *Watts.*
Salvation.

SALVATION! oh, the joyful sound!
  'Tis pleasure to our ears;
A sovereign balm for every wound,
  A cordial for our fears.
2 Buried in sorrow and in sin,
  At hell's dark door we lay!
But we arise by grace divine
  To see a heavenly day.
3 Salvation! let the echo fly
  The spacious earth around,

While all the armies of the sky
Conspire to raise the sound.

317   C. M.   *Parkinson's Sele*
A Parting Hymn.

BLESSED be the dear uniting love
That will not let us part!
Our bodies may far off remove,—
We still are joined in heart.

2 Joined in one spirit to our Head,
Where he appoints we'll go,
And still in Jesus' footsteps tread
And show his praise below.

3 Oh, let us ever walk in him,
And nothing know beside;
Nothing desire, nothing esteem.
But Jesus crucified.

4 Closer and closer let us cleave
To his beloved embrace;
With joy and gratitude receive
The fulness of his grace.

5 Oh, let us hasten to the day
Which shall our flesh restore;
When death shall all be done away,
And bodies part no more.

318   C. M. (Abridged.)   *Faucet*
Pure Religion, &c.—James i. 27

RELIGION is the chief concern
Of mortals here below:

May I its great importance learn,
 Its sovereign virtue know!

2 More needful *this* than glittering wealth,
 Or aught the world bestows;
Not reputation, food, or health
 Can give us such repose.

3 *Religion* should our thoughts engage
 Amidst our youthful bloom;
'Twill fit us for declining age,
 And for the awful tomb.

EXTRACTS:

TO BE SUNG BETWEEN PRAYER AND SERMON, AND ON ANY OTHER SUITABLE OCCASION.

319   No. 1. P. M.

I HAVE sought round the verdant earth,
 For unfading joy;
I have tried every source of mirth,
 But all, all will cloy.
Lord, bestow on me grace to set my spirit free:
Thine the praise shall be, mine, mine the joy.

No. 2. C. M.

THROUGH many dangers, toils and snares,
 I have already come;
'Tis grace has brought me safe thus far,
 And grace will lead me home.

2 The Lord has promised good to me;
 His word my hope secures;

He will my shield and portion be,
  As long as life endures.

No. 3. S. M.

GRACE led my roving feet,
  To tread the heavenly road ;
And new supplies, each hour, I meet,
  While pressing on to God.

2 Grace all the work shall crown,
  Through everlasting days;
It lays in heaven the topmost stone,
  And well deserves the praise.

No. 4. C. M.

WHY was I made to hear thy voice,
  And enter while there's room,
When thousands make a wretched choice,
  And rather starve than come.

2 'Twas the same love that spread the feast,
  That sweetly forced us in;
Else we had still refused to taste,
  And perished in our sin.

No. 5. S. M.

NOR earth, nor all the sky,
  Can one delight afford ;
No, not a drop of real joy,
  Without thy presence, Lord.

Thou art the sea of love
  Where all my pleasures roll;
The circle where my passions move,
  And center of my soul.

No. 6. C. M.

DANGERS stand thick thro' all the ground,
  To push us to the tomb;
And fierce diseases wait around,
  To hurry mortals home!

2 Good God! on what a slender thread,
  Hang everlasting things!
The eternal states of all the dead,
  Upon life's feeble strings!

No. 7. L. M.

FAR from my thoughts, vain world, be gone,
  Let my religious hours alone;
Fain would my eyes my Savior see,
I wait a visit, Lord, from thee.

No. 8. 7s.

LET me love thee more and more,
  If I love at all, I pray;
If I have not loved before,
  Help me to begin to-day.

DEATH AND THE RESURRECTION.

320   8s, 7s. *Christian Psalmist.*

ANGELS ministered to Jesus,
  When the subtle tempter fled
From the mountain of temptation,
  When his dart had vainly sped:
Down to earth they fly from heaven,
  See, what crowds are gathered round,

And the scene of his fierce trial
  Now becometh hallowed ground.

2 Angels ministered to Jesus,
    In the garden, when he lay
  Praying unto God his Father,
    That the cup might pass away:
  He was strengthened there to drink it
    For our fallen guilty race,
  And his follower's purest feelings
    Linger round that sacred place.

3 Angels ministered to Jesus
    On the morn he left the tomb,
  When the dawn of day eternal
    Burst upon its cheerless gloom;
  Down they struck the fearful soldiers,
    Rolled the massive stone away,
  And behold in death's dominions,
    Life now holds its sovereign sway.

4 Angels ministered to Jesus
    When he took his upward flight
  From the world he came to ransom,
    To the glorious realms of light;
  See, they form his willing escort,
    As his chariot mounts the sky,
  And the golden gates of glory
    At their challenge open fly.

5 They will minister to Jesus
    When the skies are backward rolled,
  And revealed high in heaven,
    All the world their Judge behold :

They will gather all his children
  To their dear Redeemer's side,
Free from earth and all its sorrows,
  With him ever to abide.

321   7s, 6s.   *Vanmeter.*
Short Life, and the Vanity of earthly things.

OUR days, alas! how transient!
  How fast our moments fly!
Each whispering, as it passes,
  That we are born to die.
The wheels of time are rolling,
  And death is hastening on;
When all our earthly pleasures
  Shall be forever gone.

2 Shall we pursue such pleasures
  As fade away and die?
Can Ophir's golden treasures
  Our wishes satisfy?
Let honor, wealth and power,
  And crowns and kingdoms fall:
For there's a dying hour
  When we shall leave them all.

3 On these low grounds of sorrow.
  No lasting pleasures rise;
Nor can the fields of nature
  Afford unsullied joys;
But there's undying pleasures
  Beyond the reach of time;
And uncorrupted treasures,
  And joys that are sublime.

4 Be this my constant calling,
 And this my chief concern,
To glorify my Savior,
 And his salvation learn:
May I but feel his presence
 When I am called to die,
And through his matchless merits
 Ascend above the sky.

322 P. M. *Christian Psalmist.*
The old Church-Yard.

OH come, come with me, to the old church yard,
 I well know the path through the soft, green sward;
Friends slumber there we were wont to regard,
We'll trace out their names in the old church yard;
Oh mourn not for them, their grief is o'er.
Weep not for them, they weep no more.
For deep is their sleep, though cold and hard
Their pillow may be in the old church yard.

2 I know it seems vain when friends depart,
To breathe kind words to the broken heart;
I know that the joys of life seem marred,
When we follow our friends to the old church yard;
But were I at rest beneath yon tree,
Why sh'ould you weep, dear friends, for me?
I'm wayworn and sad, Oh why then retard
The rest that I seek in the old church yard.

3 "Our friends linger there in the sweetest repose,
Released from the world's sad bereavements and woes;
And who would not rest with the friends they regard,
In quietude sweet in the old church yard?
We'l rest in the hope of that bright day,
When beauty shall spring from the prison of clay,
When Gabriel's voice, and the trump of the Lord,
Sh'l awaken the dead in the old church yard."

4 "Oh! weep not for me, I am anxious to go
To that haven of rest where tears never flow;
I fear not to enter that dark, lonely ward;
For soon shall I rise from the old church yard;

Yes, soon shall I join that heavenly band
Of glorified souls at my Savior's right hand;
Forever to dwell in bright mansions, prepared
For the saints who shall rise from the old church yard."

323   S. M.   *Vanmeter.*
Death of an Infant.

IT was a blooming flower,
  But oh! it bloomed to fade!
Our hopes were blasted in an hour,
  And in the dust were laid.

2 Those tender cords of love
  That twine around the heart,
Not death, nor time, can e'er remove,
  Or rend the ties apart.

3 We tried, but tried in vain,
  To keep it longer here:
Our weeping eyes could not refrain
  From the parental tear.

4 But let us weep no more,
  But wipe our tears away;
Its landed on the blissful shore
  Of everlasting day!

5 Its spirit could not stay
  In such a world as ours;
For there's a clime of endless day—
  Of never-fading flowers!

6 Oh! may it be our lot,
  By God's redeeming grace,
To share its joys, and there behold
  Its sweet, angelic face!

324   P. M. *Christian Psalmist*
Farewell.

SHED not a tear o'er your fri[end],
   When I am gone, when [I am gone;]
Smile, if the slow tolling be[ll] you shall hear,
   When I am gone, I am gone.
Weep not for me when you stand by my grave,
Think of the crowns all the ransomed shall have,
Think who has died his beloved to save,
   When I am gone, I am gone.

2 Plant ye a tree which may wave over me,
   When I am gone, when I am gone;
Sing ye a song when my grave ye shall see,
   When I am gone, I am gone.
Come at the close of a bright summer day,
Come, when the sun sheds his last lingering ray,
Come and rejoice that I thus passed away,
   When I am gone, I am gone.

3 Plant ye a rose that may bloom o'er my bed,
   When I am gone, when I am gone;
Breathe not a sigh for the blest early dead,
   When I am gone, I am gone.
Praise ye the Lord, that I'm freed from all care,
Serve ye the Lord, that my bliss ye may share,
Look up on high, and believe I am there,
   When I am gone, I am gone.

325   S. M.   *Vanmeter.*
In the Grave.

MY body's now at rest,
   My soul has fled on high,

DEATH AND THE RESURRECTION.

To dwell in mansions of the blest.
　　　　　eternity.

　　　rrows I have come.
　　　gers I have passed;
But now I'm safely landed home,
　And shall forever rest.

3 Once I was lost in sin,
　　With guilt and fear oppressed;
　But Jesus' blood has washed me clean.
　　And now I am at rest.

4 Let kingdoms rise and fall,
　　Let wars the nations waste;
　Let thunders rock this earthly ball.
　　But I shall be at rest.

5 The miseries I endured,
　　Did but a moment last;
　But Jesus hath for me secured
　　An everlasting rest.

6 My soul no more annoyed,
　　No more with sin oppressed,
　But in the presence of its God,
　　Shall now forever rest!

326　　　　L. M.　　　　*Anon.*

Sleeping in Jesus.

ASLEEP in Jesus! blessed sleep,
　From which none ever wake to weep!
A calm and undisturbed repose,
Unbroken by the last of foes.

2 Asleep in Jesus! O, how sweet,
To be for such a slumber meet!
With holy confidence to sing,
That death has lost his cruel sting.

3 Asleep in Jesus! peaceful rest,
Whose waking is supremely blest;
No fear, no wo shall dim that hour
That manifests the Savior's power.

4 Asleep in Jesus! O, for me
May such a blissful refuge be;
Securely shall my ashes lie,
Waiting the summons from on high.

5 Asleep in Jesus! far from thee
Thy kindred and their graves may be;
But there is still a blessed sleep
From which none ever wake to weep.

327   C. M.   *Vanmeter.*
The Grave-yard.

COME, thoughtless mortals, and behold
   The mansions of the dead!
Here lies the dust of young and old,
   And here you must be laid.

2 Behold the little mansion where
   The smiling infant lies;
And lo! its mother, see just there
   A grave of larger size.

3 The high, the low, the rich, the poor,
   The great and small are here;
Alike confined, and shall no more
   With living men appear.

4 Here lies the aged—there the youth,
  Who died amidst his bloom!
Here lies the saint that loved the truth,
  And there's the sinner's tomb!

5 Reflect, oh! man, as you pass by
  These mansions of the dead;
Reflect that you, also, must die,
  And make this clay your bed!

6 Have you a hope beyond the grave?
  Have you to Jesus fled?
Whose powerful arm alone can save,
  And rescue from the dead!

228 8s, 7s. *Christian Psalmist.*

SISTER, thou wast mild and lovely,
  Gentle as the summer's breeze,
Pleasant as the air of evening,
  When it floats among the trees.

2 Peaceful be thy silent slumber,
  Peaceful in the grave so low;
Thou no more will join our number,
  Thou no more our songs shalt know.

3 Dearest sister, thou hast left us,
  Here thy loss we deeply feel;
But 'tis God that hath bereft us,
  He can all our sorrows heal.

4 Yet again we hope to meet thee,
  When the day of life is fled;
Then in heaven with joy to greet thee,
  Where no farewell tear is shed.

DEATH AND THE RESURRECTION.

829 C. M. *Vanmeter*
Death.

THE monster, Death, sweeps o'er the land,
  For young nor old he saves;
Nor rich nor poor escape his hand,
  But hasten to their graves.

2 One day the smiling infant falls
  Beneath his heavy chains;
And next the aged man he calls,
  And o'er the earth he reigns.

3 'Tis thus vain man forsakes the earth,
  His life, a fleeting breath!
One day gives to the creature birth,
  The next proclaims his death!

4 Oh, transient life! inconstant world!
  When will vain mortals learn
To know their fatal destiny,
  And what's their chief concern?

5 Great God! prepare us by thy grace,
  For joys at thy right hand;
Then cheerfully we'll run our race,
  And wait for thy command.

6 If thou be with us when we die,
  In triumph we shall sing:
"O, grave! where is thy victory?
  O, death! where is thy sting?"

830 S. M. *Christian Psalmist.*
Sing to me of Heaven.

O, SING to me of heaven,
  When I am called to die;

DEATH AND THE RESURRECTION.

Sing songs of holy ecstasy,
  To waft my soul on high.

2 When cold and sluggish drops,
    Roll off my dying brow;
  Break forth in songs of joyfulness,
    Let heaven begin below.

3 When my last moments come,
    Oh! smooth my dying face;
  And catch the bright seraphic gleam,
    That on my features plays.

4 Assembled round my bed,—
    Let one loud song be given;
  Let music cheer me last on earth,
    And greet me first in heaven.

5 Then close my sightless eyes,
    And lay me down to rest;
  And clasp my cold and clammy hands
    Upon my lifeless breast.

6 Around my lifeless clay,
    Assemble those I love;
  And sing of heaven—delightful heaven,
    My glorious home above.

331   C. M.   *Christian Psalmist.*

WHEN blooming youth is snatched away
    By death's relentless hand,
  Our hearts the mournful tribute pay,
    Which pity must demand.

2 While pity prompts the rising sigh,
    O, may this truth, imprest

DEATH AND THE RESURRECTION.

With awful power, "I too must die!"
   Sink deep in every breast.

3 Let this vain world engage no more;
   Behold the gaping tomb!
It bids its us seize the present hour:
   To-morrow death may come.

4 The voice of this alarming scene,
   May every heart obey:
Nor be the heavenly warning vain,
   Which calls to watch and pray.

5 Oh, let us fly—to Jesus fly,
   Whose powerful arm can save;
Then shall our hopes ascend on high,
   And triumph o'er the grave.

332   C. M.   *Vanmeter.*
At the Loss of a Wife.

YE vanities of time, begone,
   Let me indulge my tears;
Forbid me not to mourn for one
   Who shared my hopes and fears.

2 I've lost—and oh! the painful thought
   Still lingers in my breast—
I've lost my spouse, to find her not,
   And none can give me rest.

3 She took a share in all my grief,
   And doubled all my joy;
And often gave me sweet relief,
   When troubles did annoy.

4 The memory of her virtues still
    Entwine my broken heart;
And none the vacancy can fill,
    Since death bade her depart.

5 But why, oh! why should I thus grieve,
    And mourn as others do,
Who have no hope beyond the grave,
    No better world in view?

6 Far from this vain, delusive clime,
    Of mixed, uncertain joy,
She's gone, I trust, to joys sublime,
    Eternal and on high!

333   C. M.   *Vanmeter.*
Death of an Aged Pilgrim.

BEHOLD the calm, the peaceful death,
    The aged pilgrim dies;
In Jesus he resigns his breath,
    And soars above the skies!

2 Here lies a man whose pilgrimage
    Was long and full of years,
When God was pleased to call the sage
    From this low vale of tears.

3 Weak was his body, sound his mind,
    His eyes were growing dim;
Almost a stranger to mankind,
    And they almost to him.

4 His eyes had seen the raging war;
    Beheld returning peace;

Had witnessed stern adversity,
    Prosperity and ease.

5 The world had grown a tiresome place,
    Of false, deceitful charms;
  He longed to see his Savior's face,
    And dwell in Jesus' arms.

6 And when his destined hour was come,
    Contented and resigned,
  He left his clay for heaven, his home,
    Without a look behind!

334   11s.   *Christian Psalmist.*
         Repose.

MY rest is in heaven—my home is not here,
Then why should I murmur when trials appear;
Be hushed my sad spirit—the worst that can come,
But shortens thy journey, and hastens thee home.

2 A pilgrim and stranger, I seek not my bliss,
Nor lay up my treasures in regions like this;
I look for a mansion which hands have not piled,—
I long for a city by sin undefiled.

3 Though foes and afflictions my progress oppose,
They only make heaven more sweet at the close;
Come joy or come sorrow—the worst may befall,
One moment in glory makes up for them all.

4 The thorn and the thistle around me may grow,
I would not repose me on roses below;
I ask not my portion—I seek not my rest,
Till seated with Jesus, I lean on his breast.

5 No scrip for my journey—no staff in my hand,
A pilgrim impatient I press to the land;
The path may be rugged, it cannot be long—
With hope I'll beguile it, and cheer it with song.

TIME AND ETERNITY.

335 C. M. *Vanmeter.*
The Stream of Time.

THERE is a stream whose current flows
　As ceaseless as the sun;
Onward, with sorrows, pains and woes,
　Its troubled waters run.

2 Still onward, pressing to its source—
　The ocean, whence it came;
Nor stayed by circumstance nor force,
　Is this resistless stream.

3 On its broad bosom as it glides,
　Are heedless mortals borne;
And in the boundless ocean hides
　The friends for whom we mourn.

4 The high, the low, are swept away,
　The youth, in all his prime;
The meek, the mournful and the gay,
　By the great *Stream of Time!*

5 Eternity! unfathomed sea!
　Where all our thoughts are drowned!
As boundless as infinity!
　Thither this stream is bound.

6 Soon shall its current land us there,
　Soon shall our days be o'er;
And the arch-angel shall declare
　That *Time shall be no more!*

336   L. M.   *Christian Psalmist.*

ETERNITY is just at hand,
And shall I waste my ebbing sand?
And careless view departing day,
And throw my inch of time away?

2 Be this my chief, my only care—
My high pursuit—my ardent prayer—
An interest in the Savior's blood,
My pardon sealed, and peace with God.

3 But should my brightest hopes be vain.
The rising doubts, how sharp the pain:
My fears, O gracious God, remove,
Confirm my title to thy love.

4 Search, Lord—O search my inmost heart.
And light, and hope, and joy impart:
From guilt and error set me free,
And guide me safe to heaven and thee.

337   C. M. (Abridged.)   *Watts.*
The Vanity of Man as Mortal.

TEACH me the measure of my days.
  Thou Maker of my frame;
I would survey life's narrow space
  And learn how frail I am.

2 A span is all that we can boast.
  An inch or two of time;
Man is but vanity and dust
  In all his flower and prime.

3 What should I wish or wait for, then.
  From creatures, earth, and dust?

They make our expectations vain,
 And disappoint our trust.

4 Now I forbid my carnal hope,
 My fond desires recall;
 I give my mortal interest up,
 And make my God my all.

MISCELLANEOUS.

338 11s. *Anon.*

The Bride, the Lamb's Wife.

BEHOLD! a sweet wonder in heaven was seen!
 The Bride of the Lamb, a most beautiful queen!
The truth, like a garment, so fair to behold,
Adorned her with hangings much brighter than gold!

2 And clothed with the sun of God's love, she must be
A wonder in heaven, a beauty to see!
A wonder, indeed, since Jehovah on high
Has called her his bride from all eternity.

3 Before the foundation of heaven was laid,
 He owned his affection for this comely maid;
 Betrothed her and called her to be his Son's wife,
 Who, freely, to save her, did lay down his life,

4 He crowns her with glory, makes justice her seat;
 The body of law he puts under her feet;
 To travel the precepts to Jesus' arms,
 He crowns her with glory, in smiling, sweet charms.

5 The ancient twelve patriarchs bow to behold,
 All shining in glory much brighter than gold,
 And thousands of angels, whose garments are clean,
 All filled with wonder, admiring the Queen.

6 The wedding is ready, the Bridegroom won't stay,
 The attendants are chosen, and will not delay;
 The lamb it is slain, and the supper is found,
 And the wine is prepared on the table all around.

INDEX TO SUBJECTS.

	HYMNS.
God, His Being and Attributes,	1—25
The Fall,	26—36
The Scriptures,	37—44
The Law,	45—54
The Gospel,	55—71
Christ His Divinity and Incarnation,	72—81
Christ His Birth,	82—84
Christ His Life and Characters,	85-120
Christ His Sufferings and Death,	121-136
Christ's Resurrection and Ascension,	137-141
Christ's Intercession,	142-146
Union with Christ,	147-152
Predestination and Election,	153-161
Salvation and Redemption,	162-175
Justification,	176-182
Forgiveness and Pardon,	183-188
Regeneration and Conversion,	189-196
Invitations and Promises,	197-208
The Christian,	209-241
Heavenly Prospects,	242-252
Faith,	253-256
Hope,	257-259
Love to God,	260-263
Brotherly Love,	264-267
The Church,	268-275
Reception of Members,	276-284
Baptism,	285-292
The Lord's Supper,	293-300
Before Preaching,	301-310
Closing Hymns,	311-318
Tracts,	319
Death and the Resurrection,	320-334
Time and Eternity,	335-337
Miscellaneous,	338-345

MISCELLANEOUS.

345   7s.   *Vann.*

ACROSTIC.

I WAS almost in despair,
S inking down with grief and fear;
A ll my sins around me rose,
A s so many mighty foes.

2 C onscious of my lost estate,
N ow I thought it was too late!
V ain I saw my life had been,
A ll unholy and unclean.

3 N othing had my hands to give;
M ercy did my spirit crave;
E ndless life, the Lord bestowed:
T hus a wretch was brought to God.

4 E verlasting praise shall rise,
R ighteous sovereign of the skies,
  To thy name, for such displays
  Of thy rich and sovereign grace.

INDEX

TO THE
FIRST LINES OF THE HYMNS.

	HYMN.
Adam, our father and our head	27
A home in heaven! what a joyful thought	248
Alas! and did my Savior bleed	127
All powerful, self-existent God!	3
Amazing grace! how sweet the sound!	222
Am I a soldier of the cross?	209
And let this feeble body fail	351
And yet, the Lord remembers me	214
Angels ministered to Jesus	320
Arise, my soul, arise	146
A body when the soul has fled	255
Asleep in Jesus! blessed sleep!	326
A sacred union we behold	150
As on the cross the Savior hung	128
Awaked by Sinai's awful sound	190
Awakened soul, to Jesus fly	209
Awake, my heart, arise, my tongue	182
Awake, my tongue, thy tribute bring	20
Awake, our souls, and bless his name	99
Awake, sweet gratitude, and sing	142
Backward, with humble shame, we look	80
Before Jehovah's awful throne	28
Before the covenant angel's face	179
Begin, my soul, the heavenly song	343
Begin, my tongue, some heavenly theme	198
Behold! a sinner, dearest Lord	207
Behold! a sweet wonder in heaven was seen	339
Behold! how Adam's helpless race	54
Behold! the calm, the peaceful death	338
Behold! the gift of God	93
Behold! the mount of Zion	270
Behold the sure foundation stone	108
Behold! the woman's promised seed	70
Behold! what wondrous love	235
Believing soul, why tarriest thou?	288
Beneath the sacred throne of God	172
Beside the gospel pool	207

INDEX TO FIRST LINES.

Blest be the everlasting God	141
Blest be the tie that binds	264
Blest be the dear uniting love	317
Blessed with the joys of innocence	26
Blood has a voice to pierce the skies	133
Blow ye the trumpet, blow	64
Bound by the cords of love	266
Brethren, I am come again	307
Brethren, while we sojourn here	230
Broad is the road and wide the gate	308
But few among the carnal wise	161
Children of the heavenly King	149
Christ and his cross is all our theme	63
Christ is the way to heavenly bliss	101
Come, all ye humble pilgrims,	232
Come, dearest Lord, who reigns above	57
Come, Holy Spirit, come	304
Come, Holy Spirit, heavenly Dove	305
Come, humble sinner, in whose breast	282
Come in, ye blessed of our God	280
Come see the Lord's annointed King	84
Come, thou fount of every blessing	215
Come, thou long expected Jesus	98
Come, thoughtless mortals, and behold	327
"Come unto me," the Savior calls	206
Come, we that love the Lord	240
Come, ye beloved of the Lord	290
Compared with Christ, in all beside	90
Convinced, as a sinner, to Jesus I came	119
Dark and thorny is the desert	236
Dear Lord, and will thy pardoning love	289
Dear Lord, though bitter is the cup	217
Dearest of all the names above	89
Dear Savior, we are thine	151
Deep in the dust before thy throne	29
Deep in our hearts let us record	121
Depraved minds on ashes feed	95
Desponding believer, come hold up thy head	283
Dismiss us with thy blessing, Lord	311
Distressed soul to Jesus go	202
Do not frustrate the grace of God	49
Do not I love thee, O my Lord	260
Enslaved by sin and bound in chains	162
Eternal, ere the worlds were made	155

INDEX TO FIRST LINES.

Eternal God! almighty Cause	1
Eternity is just at hand	336
Expand my soul, arise and sing	154
Extracts	319
Father of mercies, in thy word	40
Faith is the brightest evidence	253
Faith, 'tis a precious grace	256
Far from my thoughts vain world begone	301
Forgiveness! 'tis a joyful sound	184
From all that dwell below the skies	314
From every stormy wind that blows	306
From Sinai's Mount to Zion's hill	53
From whence doth this union arise	267
Full of vain thoughts and worldly cares	211
God, in the riches of his grace	168
God is a Spirit, just and wise	22
God moves in a mysterious way	12
God with us! O, glorious name	75
"Go preach my gospel," saith the Lord	60
Grace, 'tis a charming sound	173
Great God! 'tis from thy sovereign grace	174
Great God, with wonder and with praise	42
Great Salem's King, of old renowned	66
Had I the tongues of Greeks and Jews	263
Hail, sovereign love, that first began	110
Hail, the blest morn, when the great mediator	82
Happy the church, thou sacred place	268
Hark, my soul! it is the Lord	261
Have you heard, have you heard of that heavenly clime?	294
He dies, the Friend of sinners, dies	125
He lives, the great Redeemer, lives	143
Here, Lord, my soul convicted stands	47
Holy Bible! book divine	37
How beauteous are their feet	62
How can a sinner stand before	181
How can I be a child of grace	225
How cold and barren is my soul	218
How did my heart rejoice to hear	271
How firm a foundation, ye saints of the Lord	233
How happy are they	281
How lost was my condition	196
How oft, alas! this wretched heart	187
How pleasing to behold and see	298
How precious is the Book divine	89

INDEX TO FIRST LINES.

How shall I my Savior set forth	73
How sweet and awful is the place	294
How sweet the name of Jesus sounds	112
How tedious and tasteless the hours	231
Hungry, and faint, and poor	203
I am a miracle of grace	178
I am a stranger here below	210
"I am the bread of life"	94
I came to the spot where the White Pilgrim lay	340
"If ye love me," says Christ, the Lord	284
I looked, and lo! an awful gulf beneath	342
I love thy kingdom, Lord	272
I'm almost gone! just on the eve	344
I'm bound for New Jerusalem	244
I'm not ashamed to own my Lord	276
In Adam's loins, by sin we fell	28
In all my troubles sharp and strong	257
In all my vast concerns with thee	4
In Christ, I've all my soul's desire	92
In eighteen hundred thirty-three	339
In evil, long I took delight	195
Infinite grief! amazing wo	135
In union with the Lamb	148
In your great Master's holy name	59
I send the joys of earth away	302
I sing the almighty power of God	10
Is there no shelter from the wrath	186
It was a blooming flower	323
I was almost in despair	345
Jehovah reigns, his throne is high	16
Jerusalem, my happy home	245
Jesus, and shall it ever be	291
Jesus, hail, enthroned in glory	144
Jesus hath magnified the law	180
Jesus, I my cross have taken	292
Jesus, I sing thy matchless grace	108
Jesus, my all, to heaven is gone	116
Jesus, my love, my chief delight	106
Jesus! O, what a wondrous theme,	102
Jesus, the sum and substance is	61
Jesus, the heavenly lover, gave	96
Jesus, thou art the sinner's Friend	183
Jesus, thy blood and righteousness	177
Jesus, we bless thy Father's name	153

INDEX TO FIRST LINES. v

Jesus, with all thy saints above	165
Joy to the world! the Lord is come	80
Keep silence, all created things	5
Laden with sin and guilt am I	204
Laden with guilt, and full of fears	43
Let every saint employ his tongue	88
Let me, my Savior and my God	156
Let the wild leopards of the wood	86
Let others compass seas and lands	309
Let the whole race of creatures lie	158
Let those who inhabit the Rock	51
Like Noah's weary dove	278
Like sheep we went astray	131
Look down with wonder and surprise	124
Lord, at thy table I behold	296
Lord, can a soul like mine	218
Lord, dost thou show a corner-stone	109
Lord, how mysterious are thy ways	24
Lord, thou hast searched and seen me through	7
Lord, we adore thy vast designs	18
Lord, we are blind, we mortals, blind	15
Lord, unto whom should sinners go	97
Lord, who can be sufficient	65
Lo! the stone is rolled away	187
Lo! what an entertaining sight	265
May the grace of Christ, our Savior	312
My body's now at rest	325
My God, my life, my love	289
My rest is in heaven, my home is not here	384
My Savior, let me hear thy voice	185
My Savior on Mount Calvary	134
My sorrows, like a flood	188
No more, my God, I boast no more	171
Now begin the heavenly theme	163
Now let my soul, with wonder, trace	288
Now to the Lord, a noble song	77
Not all the nobles of the earth	220
Not all the outward forms on earth	191
Of all the joys we mortals know	113
Oh! come, come with me to the old church-yard	322
Oh! for a closer walk with God	228
Oh! for a glance of heavenly day	310
Oh! painful truth, it is to tell	81
O! how delightful is the theme	120

INDEX TO FIRST LINES.

O! how melodious was that voice	228
O! land of rest, for thee I sing	252
Once more we come before our God	303
"One thing is needful," saith the Lord	107
On Jordan's stormy banks I stand	243
On the brink of fiery ruin	192
On Zion, his most holy mount	70
On Zion's sacred mount I saw	167
O! sing to me of heaven	330
O! Spirit, guide my pen	11
O! the Almighty Lord	21
Our days, alas! how transient	321
Our father lost his innocence	35
O! what amazing words of grace	197
People of the living God	279
Pity a helpless sinner, Lord	300
Poor, weak and worthless though I am	105
Precious Bible! what a treasure	88
"Proclaim my Gospel," saith the Lord	55
Raise your triumphant songs	81
Redemption! O, the joyful news!	164
Religion is the chief concern	318
Religion! what a vast estate!	318
Rock of ages, shelter me	118
Salvation, how precious the sound	170
Salvation, O. the joyful sound	316
Salvation, what a heavenly theme	166
Savior, visit thy plantation	275
Shall wisdom cry aloud?	117
Shall we go on to sin?	175
Shed not a tear o'er your friend's early bier	324
Show pity, Lord, O, Lord forgive	208
Sin is the only evil thing	88
Sin, like a venomous disease	32
Sinners, rejoice, it's Christ that died	136
Sinners, this solemn truth regard	189
Sister, thou wast mild and lovely	323
Soon as the Son of God had made	85
Sovereign Ruler of the skies	157
Stranger, if thou wantest to know	193
Teach me the measure of my days	337
Tell me no more of earthly toys	219
Tell me, Savior, from above	115
The angels that watched round the tomb	189

INDEX TO FIRST LINES.

Thee, we adore, eternal Word	74
The finest flower that ever blowed	129
The fool, with impudence	6
The glories of my Lord were told	91
The glorious gospel of our God	58
The glorious Son of God	285
The God of my salvation lives	258
The gospel brings tidings to each wounded soul	71
The holy spirit must renew	69
The King of heaven his table spreads	297
The law and gospel both agree	48
The law by Moses came	67
The law commands and makes us know	45
The law of God is just	50
The Lord declares his will	46
The Lord is come, the heavens proclaim	78
The Lord of life his table spread	299
The monster, death, sweeps o'er the land	829
The name of Jesus is my trust	241
The name of the Lord is my tower of defence	100
The Saint of God how highly blest	221
The Savior sent the gospel forth	68
The spacious firmament on high	9
There is a land of pure delight	250
There is a fountain filled with blood	104
There is a period known to God	160
There is a stream whose current flows	335
There is a spot to me more dear	194
There's not a tint that paints the rose	8
Though sin and satan both unite	216
Thus far my God hath led me on	226
Thus was the great Redeemer plunged	286
Thy way, O, God, is in the sea	17
'Tis by the faith of joys to come	254
'Tis a point I long to know	224
"'Tis finished!" so the Savior cried	130
'Tis grace, free grace, eternal grace	169
'Tis midnight, and on Olive's brow	122
'Tis religion that can give	315
'Tis the Bridegroom's voice I hear	152
To banquet once the spouse was led	262
To Christ, the Lord, let every tongue	86
'Twas by an order from the Lord	41
'Twas far above the earth I fixed mine eyes	247

INDEX TO FIRST LINES.

'Twas fixed in God's eternal mind	159
'Twas on that dark, that doleful night	298
'Twixt Jesus and the chosen race	147
Unto us a child is born	76
Vain are the hopes the sons of men	176
Wait, O, my soul, thy Maker's will	14
Water from salvation's wells	205
We are a garden walled around	273
Well, the Redeemer's gone	145
Were oceans, rivers, floods and lakes	25
We sing the amazing deeds	295
We've no abiding city here	242
We speak of the realms of the blast	246
What is our God, or what his name	2
What if we read and understand	44
What heavenly comfort do we find	237
What little comfort do we find	229
What lonely band is this I see	287
What think ye of Christ? is the test	72
What strange perplexities arise	212
What wondrous love is this	284
When all thy mercies I survey	227
When at a distance, Lord, we trace	87
When blooming youth is snatched away	331
When from the precepts to the cross	52
When I can read my title clear	277
When I survey the wondrous cross	126
When I the holy grave survey	140
When Jacob, the pilgrim, was wearied by day	111
When man transgressed the law of God	84
When on the cross my Savior died	132
While in the vale of vision dead	56
While my Redeemer's near	114
While shepherds watched their flocks by night	83
Why should the Lord's divine decrees	19
With what unbounded power and skill	13
Ye burdened souls, to Jesus come	199
Ye children of Zion and saints of the Lord	341
Ye humble souls that seek the Lord	138
Ye vanities of time, begone	332
Yonder amazing sight I see	123
You may sing the beauties of mountain and dale	274
Your harps, ye trembling saints	259
Zion's a city God hath blessed	269

ERRATA.

Hymn 7, for S. M. read L. M.
Hymn 25, second line read "name of water."
Hymn 37, read 2 Tim., iii, 16.
Hymn 53, for L. M. read C. M.
Hymn 101, second line, erase "is."
Hymn 112, for L. M. read C. M.
Hymn 114, for L. M. read S. M.
Hymn 123, for L. M. read C. M.
Hymn 167, third verse, read "blood-bought."
Hymn 177, third verse, read *bold* not behold.
Hymn 181, fourth verse, read "The sinner."
Hymn 295, for L. M. read S. M.
Hymn 308, for C. M. read L. M.
Hymn 328 wrongly printed 228.

TO MY PATRONS.

I beg leave to say, that the long delay in the forth-coming of this work has been owing, entirely, to unavoidable delays in printing.

Send on your orders, now, kind friends, and they shall be promptly filled. The price first proposed—of Sixty Cents per copy, sent free—will barely cover cost, but I shall trust to the liberality of brethren to remunerate me for time and trouble.

Address, with Post Office Orders,
    I. N. VANMETER,
      Macomb, Ill.